The Lost Travel Diaries of the

LAUGHING POLICEMAN

VOLUME I.

The Lost Travel Diaries of the

LAUGHING POLICEMAN

VOLUME 1.

GLENN WOOD

ISBN: 978-1-0670744-1-8

LAUGHING BOOKS

INTRODUCTION

I'm Glenn Wood, also known as The Laughing Policeman, due to the popular autobiographies I wrote about my brief and disastrous career in the New Zealand Police.

I'm an author, copywriter, screenwriter, dad (unpaid), podcaster (isn't everyone) and travel writer.

After my police memoirs, I deviated into the world of children's books. This change of direction garnered me considerably less acclaim than you might think, mainly because kids seem to have stopped reading, but also because I live in New Zealand, an extremely small market where humans are vastly outnumbered by sheep.

Unfortunately, our woolly farmyard friends are not big readers, especially of the children's genre. (They prefer thrillers. Big Jack Reacher fans.)

Aside from writing for kids, I also love travel writing and have had several articles published in various magazines over the years. I'd largely forgotten about these pieces until I recently came across one in a pile of old magazines in a dentist's waiting room. I mean, seriously, get some more up-to-date magazines. Judging by my dental bill, you can afford it!

It was fun revisiting both the article and my memories of the destination it pertained to and it inspired me to rootle around in the dark corners of my home to see what else I could unearth. Buried deep in long forgotten boxes, I came across a series of half-written travel diaries chronicling a lifetime's worth of globe-trotting.

Two things struck me. I'd been to some interesting places and my travels were filled with the kind of personal misfortunes and missteps that people enjoyed in my police memoirs.

Readers of those books will know that my career in the constabulary was dogged by poor decision-making and bad luck. My travel experiences follow a similar pattern. For its part, the universe seems to enjoy lobbing obstacles and adversity my way, normally with unexpected and humorous results, for everyone else.

Having unearthed these forgotten diaries, it seemed a shame not to finish the stories and share them. Thus, this book was born.

Within its pages you'll be taken, dear reader, into the hostile depths of the Bornean jungle; you'll be exposed to the perils of travelling in Northern Ireland during 'The Troubles', then discover ancient Mayan temples and exotic wildlife in Belize and Guatemala, before heading behind enemy lines in Vietnam, and more besides.

All without leaving the comfort and safety of your home, which would have been a far more sensible course for me.

It's fair to say I never let the truth get in the way of a good story. None of the stories in these pages are made up, but I'll happily pitch in exaggeration and questionable recollection for dramatic or comic effect. I make no apology for that. I'd rather be entertaining than accurate. If you want precision, read a map.

I haven't changed any names to protect the innocent because, let's face it, none of them are.

This book, like my travel, is unstructured and plays fast and loose with chronology and timelines. Like a Time Lord, if you will.

Two quick notes before we begin.

Eula, my darling wife, passed away in 2021 from a brain tumour. She was my life and travel partner and appears frequently in this book. Eula made every trip we went on immeasurably better. She knew some of my more stupidly dangerous adventures were not for her, but never stood in my way (though she probably should have). I love her dearly and miss her every day. Writing about her is heart-wrenching and uplifting in equal measure.

And finally. This book features some surfing content and discussion, mainly because I'm a surfer and this informed some of my travel decisions. I have kept these stories to a minimum and have done my best to ensure they are entertaining and amusing. Rest assured, there is more than enough non-surf-related content to keep everyone happy.

I hope you enjoy these recently unearthed travel tales. I loved having them.

Glenn Wood aka The Laughing Policeman.

CHAPTER ONE

THE LUCKY COUNTRY. PART ONE

Australia—June-ish 1980s (but still worryingly relevant today). Diary lost on a plane, (How does that even happen?) so I'm relying mostly on memory and creative license.

Ahh, Australia.

How we Kiwis love to hate you. But also, kinda love you. It's a typical big brother, little brother relationship.

Australians, on the other hand, don't give a rip what we think. That's probably because they are too busy trying to stay alive. Australia has more things that can kill you than almost any other country in the world and that's excluding actual Australians. It contains the most animals with the deadliest venom, including box jellyfish, stonefish, blue-ringed octopus (which no sane person would want as their teacher) and bizarrely, the world's deadliest snail.

Yes, you heard that right. Snail.

Sure, it's not likely to chase you down and kill you, but the marbled cone snail shoots out a poison-laden harpoon that contains enough venom to kill a grown man. In fact, just a few microlitres of cone snail toxin is enough to kill ten people.

The good news continues.

The sting is painless so you don't know you've been stung, well, not until you experience numbness, tingling, and possibly death; at which point you might catch on. The harpoon-like stinger can also penetrate wetsuit material, so if you pick up the pretty shell assuming it's harmless, your dive gloves will offer no protection. Naturally, there is no antivenom for cone snail stings. Good, oh.

Just by scratching the surface, we have discovered possible death by jellyfish, octopus and aquatic snails. Okay, Australia, what else have you got?

Quite a bit, as it turns out.

Twenty of the twenty-five most venomous snakes in the world live in The Lucky Country, including the inland taipan, which grabs the number one spot. Well done, that slippery death-bringer.

Cassowaries, which run free in Queensland, have been listed in the Guinness Book of Records as the world's most dangerous bird, with this charming assessment done in 1958 by ornithologist Thomas E Gillard; *'The inner or second of the three toes is fitted with a long, straight, murderous nail which can sever an arm or eviscerate an abdomen with ease.'*

Excellent. Evisceration is a great word to have associated with something that can outrun you.

Then we have saltwater crocodiles, the cuddliest of nature's surviving dinosaurs.

During one memorable trip to Cairns, my wife and I were staying at the upmarket Sheraton Grand Mirage Resort in Port Douglas. Confident in four-star luxury and security, I prepared myself for a relaxing swim in the labyrinth of beautiful, crystal-clear pools that wound through the resort. Just as I was about to dive in, the hotel manager ambled past.

"Be a bit careful going round the corners Cobber, we've had a few salties in over the last few weeks," he drawled casually.

What the actual!

He was telling me there was a reasonable chance I could swim into a saltwater crocodile in the hotel pool. It'd be great. We could have a chat about the weather, share a laugh about the German tourists pinching the best sun loungers. Then it would clamp its jaws around my torso and spin me into a bloody roll of death—completely ruining my swimming goggles.

I did have a swim, but it wasn't the most relaxing dip I've ever had. Only bettered a few days later when I was swimming a bit further down the coast. As I emerged from the sea, my wife pointed out a sign which I'd missed, politely warning of crocodiles in the area.

Seriously, Australia, if you are going to advise stupid tourists about potentially life-ending hazards, at least make your sign clearly visible. How about using three-metre-high flashing neon letters that say something like:

DO NOT SWIM HERE BECAUSE AN ANCIENT SHARP-TOOTHED BEAST MAY RISE FROM THE DEPTHS AND TERMINATE YOUR EXISTENCE.

Maybe have a siren going as well. I don't think that would be excessive. There is, of course, more, a lot more.

In Australia, stingray can also kill you. RIP Steve.

Dingoes pose a threat to the toddler set, and even their national animal, the kangaroo, has been known to seriously mess up innocent bystanders. Though I will say they taste great in a curry. And, because this is Australia, you can find many of the fore-mentioned creatures served up in a pie: crocodile, kangaroo and Emu for sure, though, to my knowledge, no one has put pastry around a deadly jellyfish yet. If anyone was going to do it, it would be an Australian.

To summarise, in the immortal words of the fantastic Australian comedy duo The Scared Weird Little Guys—Come to Australia. You might accidentally get killed.

Armed with none of this knowledge, I set off for my first Australian adventure in 1983. I was visiting relations who lived in Sydney. I'd never met them but assumed they'd be friendly-ish. I was travelling with a mate whose nickname was Boz. He was a tall, gangly guy I'd known since we were kids. The typical 'grew up on the same street' story.

Boz was best known for his complete lack of coordination, a trait we shared. I once saw him fall off a low wall on his motorcycle simply by not putting a stabilising foot on top of it in time. It was quite spectacular. Both he and the bike tumbled about three metres and ended in a tangled heap of man and machine in the neighbour's garden. Surprisingly, only his pride was injured.

Boz was the perfect travelling companion for me, a man also legendary as an accident waiting to happen.

Writing the account of our travels should be easy, as I kept a meticulous travel diary chronicling every day of the trip. I say 'should be' because unfortunately, I left the diary on the plane on the way home. It, quite literally, became a travelling diary (thanks to Katherine Downs for that joke). Come on Glenn! One job.

This means I'm going to have to rely on memory, so you'll have to forgive me for sketchy descriptions and events that probably loom larger in my mind than they did in real life.

I remember being excited about the trip. This was to be my first experience of overseas travel. My parents worked hard but didn't have the money to spare on excursions outside New Zealand. They are both well-travelled now, but not so during my childhood. Not that I felt I was missing out. In those days, international travel was the preserve of the rich, so it wasn't surprising our holidays were taken locally. This meant I was a travel rookie until my early twenties.

My first impressions of Australia were of size and scale, and these remain so to this day. It's a bloody big country. I remember looking out the plane window and being awestruck by the continent that stretched out before me. It's the largest country in Oceania and the world's sixth biggest in total.

Sydney was also a real city. Up to this point, I'd only lived in New Plymouth—NZ's twelfth largest city, a population of approximately forty thousand, and Palmerston North—ninth most sizeable with sixty thousand. Sydney, on the other hand, at the time had over three million people, almost the equivalent of our entire country. This was the big league.

I don't remember much about the city itself, as my cousins lived out in the suburbs. I'm not sure where, exactly. The address would have been written in my travel diary.

Boz and I were invited to their place for a BBQ; how very Australian and yes, there was shrimp on it. Barbecuing is also a Kiwi thing. We can carbonise a sausage with the best of them. The food, however, wasn't the thing that stayed with me from that night (though it stayed with me for most of the next day). It was the revelation that my cousins were Bogans, which is an antipodean form of redneck. I may just be replaying a scene from the Aussie classic movie 'The Castle' but I'm sure there was a range of large horsepower cars in the driveway, almost certainly Holdens. They also had a Pit Bull Terrier whose favourite trick was to clamp its mighty jaws around a large tree branch and then be lifted completely off the ground, hanging in the air with a death grip still on the branch. The dog didn't seem to mind, but I'm sure the branch enjoyed it less.

I made a mental note to stay on the dog's good side, deciding I'd throw it a sausage or two. I certainly wouldn't be hand-feeding it. Not after seeing those jaws at work. One slip and I'd be known as 'eight-fingered Woodsy' for the rest of my life.

The second most powerful memory was of a spider in a jar.

You probably noticed that I left two of Australia's deadly creatures off my initial list—sharks and spiders. This was no accident as they feature in upcoming stories (sharks soon—insert Jaws music here).

The glass-encased spider in question was causing a lot of excitement amongst my cousins. They couldn't wait to show it to me and inform me it had been caught in the back garden, not far from where I currently sat.

It was a highly poisonous *funnel-web spider*.

The thing was terrifying to behold, especially for someone suffering from arachnophobia, as I do. It was also very much alive. The funnel-web is everything you don't want in a spider (or, in fact, anything). It was big, pitch black, fanged, threatening, aggressive, and extremely venomous.

Before 1981, when an anti-venom was developed by a team led by Struan Sutherland in Melbourne (nice one Struan), bites from

Sydney funnel-webs resulted in thirteen documented deaths. Their fangs are large and powerful, capable of penetrating fingernails and soft shoes—I'd like to meet the person who tested this—and they have ample venom glands, which is nice because we wouldn't want them to run out, would we?

The funnel-web's bite is painful and dangerous and requires immediate medical attention, which made me wonder why my cousin was jiggling it around in the jar and really pissing it off.

"Would you like a closer look?" he said, unscrewing the lid.

I assured him I did not by emitting a high-pitched shriek and hiding behind Boz, who was surprisingly unfazed. I suggested giving it to the dog because if anyone could sort it out, it would be the pit bull, though I suspect he would have been too smart to take on the spider.

Having tormented me with the funnel-web, my relations still had one more spider-related trick up their sleeve. As I headed for the bathroom later in the evening, I was told to look out for redback spiders under the toilet seat. This is so common in Australia that some jolly wag wrote a song about it and called it 'Redback on the Toilet Seat'. No confusion there.

The song tells the story of a man bitten on the bum by a redback spider while going for an evening crap. He ends up in the hospital, but not before his wife threatens to use a cutthroat razor on him for reasons I can't quite work out. Those crazy Aussies.

Anyway, redback spiders are also known as the Australian black widow for maximum cool points. They look like they have a Game of Thrones crest on their backs (see cool points) and are slightly less deadly than the funnel-webs. That's not saying much. They are still considered highly venomous, often bite multiple times and seem to target the genitals, which is just mean.

Redbacks are responsible for between 2,000 and 10,000 bites a year across Australia and while the bites aren't usually fatal (thanks mainly to anti-venom), symptoms include nausea, vomiting, headache, agitation and, in some cases, extreme pain. All of which makes what should be a peaceful time in the lavatory the Australian equivalent of Russian roulette.

To this day, I can't go to the toilet in Australia without worrying about what might lurk under the seat.

Now, you would have thought two deadly species of spider would be enough, but not for Australia. Oh, no. There's plenty more to come.

The mouse, whitetail and recluse spiders all have potentially dangerous venom and will bite if feeling threatened, or if it's a Tuesday and they've run out of their favourite pastries at the spider bakery.

Then we have the trapdoor spider, which is a sneaky bastard as it lives in a camouflaged burrow and lies in wait for its prey, or 'keen gardeners', as they are also known.

It's hardly worth mentioning the common garden weave orb spider because their bites only cause minor pain. They make up for this by being as aggressive as an internet troll on a caffeine high. The garden weave orb wins the prize for most spider bites in Australia as well as the most unnecessarily complicated name.

The Lucky Country also has its own tarantula; of course it does. Naturally, these are huge, hairy and terrifying, though, in the context of Australian wildlife, they are considered almost friendly as their bite only causes extreme pain and won't kill you. Unless you're a dog. They can kill dogs, so clearly I'm using 'friendly' in the loosest possible way.

I've left the biggest bastard to last. The Huntsman spider.

I rate them high in the nasty spider ranking, not because of their venom (which isn't considered dangerous to humans) but because they are frigging huge, frighteningly fast, look like they've been designed by H. R. Giger and are bloody everywhere. They are also evil geniuses.

Knowing that their venom can't kill, they have devised cunning new ways to destroy humanity by using the element of surprise. The huntsman utilises shock and awe tactics by suddenly leaping out from behind innocuous household objects, dramatically increasing the likelihood of cardiac arrest for anyone in the vicinity. This tactic is particularly effective when employed in a motor vehicle. Huntsman exploding out of the dashboard or leaping from behind sun visors have been blamed for an unnerving amount of motor vehicle 'accidents'.

Weirdly, Aussies seem surprisingly immune to the danger. I have friends who have given pet names to these monsters and happily let them live in their houses.

You know who you are.

CHAPTER TWO

THE LUCKY COUNTRY. PART TWO

Australia 1983 (mostly). Diary still lost somewhere over the Pacific.

Having survived the wilds of suburban Sydney, Boz and I decided it was time to hit the beach. Not just any beach. We were heading for arguably one of Australia's most famous ones: Surfers Paradise on Queensland's Gold Coast. Bondi probably claims the 'most famous' title now due to the wacky antics of those crazy lifeguards on 'Bondi Rescue', but back in the day, Surfers gave it a good run for its money.

The reason we went to Surfers Paradise was, funnily enough, to surf. There was only one thing standing in our way—neither of us knew how. Well, that's not strictly true. I'd attempted to stand up on an old eleven-foot log in my teens, but had little success. We figured, however, there would be no better place to learn than a town which had the words 'surf' and 'paradise' in its name. Our logic was sound, and upon leaving our hotel for a quick recce, we immediately ascertained that the place did indeed have waves. All we needed now was a surfboard and someone to show us how to use it.

The smart thing to do would have been to pay for some surf lessons, but as I said, that would have been the smart thing, so there was no way that was going to happen.

Instead, we hired a board to share and learn on the fly. I mean, how hard could it be? Surfers aren't exactly known for their intellects. I'd seen blocks of surf wax before and the thing that struck me most, aside from the pleasant coconut smell, was they had DO NOT EAT written on the back in bold type. I imagine this came about because of a conversation like this:

Surfer 1: "Dude, I'm starving after that surf. Did you pack any sandwiches?"

Surfer 2: "No Dude. I thought you were doing that."

Surfer 1: "Aw Dude, what are we going to eat now?"

Surfer 2: "Hey, have you noticed that wax smells like coconut...."

And scene.

So, we hired a surfboard. It was a five-foot-nine short board and entirely inappropriate to learn on. I've now been surfing for over twenty years and still wouldn't be able to ride it. Had we even an ounce of sense we would have gone for a longer, more stable board, but we were in our early twenties and our perceived abilities far outstretched our actual ones.

With our surfboard safely hired and stashed in our hotel room, all we needed now were some waves. We rushed to the famous surf beach and prepared ourselves for perfect peeling peaks with shimmering green faces that stretched to the horizon.

It was as flat as a snake that had been run over by a cement mixer.

Boz was keen to give it a go anyway, but given his complete lack of coordination and the fact there was literally nothing to ride, we tried again the following day. Surely, this was an anomaly. All you need to surf is a board and a few waves, right? Wrong. I've discovered that surfing is one of the world's most frustrating sports. All the following things need to align perfectly before it's worth getting the board out of the car.

TIDE: You need to know which part of the tide creates the best surf conditions at the particular surf break you are going to. As a rule of thumb, an incoming mid-tide is normally good, but sadly, it's not that simple. Some surf breaks work best on high tide, some on low, others somewhere in between. They are all different and you need to know the optimum tide for any break you want to surf.

WIND: One of the most fickle and frustrating aspects of surfing. To get even a half-decent session, the wind must be blowing off shore, which means blowing off the beach towards the waves. This holds the surf up, creating clean faces for surfers to ride. If the wind is blowing on-shore, from the ocean toward the beach, this crushes the waves, turning them to white water mush. A cross-shore wind can be okay, but it tends to ruffle the surface of the water, making for a bumpy ride.

SWELL: Pretty important. If there's too little, there's nothing to ride. If there's too much, it might just kill you. You need to know what size surf you can handle for your abilities and the board you're riding. A pro-surfer can handle a ten-foot wave with ease, whereas I'm uncomfortable on anything over four feet. A short board will handle bigger surf while a longboard is designed for smaller days.

SAND BANKS: These change all the time, especially after a big swell. One day, a beach might have nice peaks everywhere, the next moment the sand moves and the peaks are gone. This is why reef breaks are so popular. They are generally more consistent and don't change.

If even one of these things is just slightly off, then you're in for a messy grovel.

With time to kill before we tried again, Boz and I took in the sights of Surfers Paradise. This consisted mainly of shops (which elicited zero interest from two financially and fashion-challenged Kiwi blokes), restaurants and high-rise apartments. Just as we were about to give up and head back to the hotel bar, we came upon something that immediately grabbed our attention. An exhibition about sharks (told you this was coming)!

Now, you'd think that a showcase of the world's deadliest marine predators would be a stupid thing to view just before embarking on your first-ever surf session and you'd be right. For reasons I still can't fathom, neither of our brains made the link. We simply thought—Sharks. Cool. In our defence, Jaws was still two years away from release and the full horror of these cold-eyed killers was yet to be unleashed on an unsuspecting public.

The shark exhibit was bone-chilling. Mainly because we didn't expect it to contain an actual embalmed sixteen-foot great white shark. I have never seen anything quite as horrifying, before or since. This monster had come out of the ocean somewhere off the Australian coast and was touring the country, just to remind everyone how vulnerable we are. The thing that struck me was the pure size of the fish. It was the length of a very large automobile, with a similar girth and a weight of somewhere around two tons.

The jaws of the beast had been opened so you could clearly see its teeth, which were like jagged, razor-sharp mini daggers about five inches long. I'm not sure how it died; I mean, the great white in *Jaws* had to be blown to bits just to slow it down. Maybe this one had a heart condition or got something stuck in its throat, like a shipping container. All I know is that whoever caught it and dragged it out of the water was insanely brave or just plain insane.

Accompanying the exhibition was a display that chronicled shark attacks in Australian waters. The statistics didn't make comfortable reading, with over six-hundred attacks since 1791 and more than one-hundred-and-eighty fatalities. This was back in the eighties. Statistics are even worse today with over a thousand attacks and over two-hundred-and-thirty deaths, although the introduction of shark nets to beaches has greatly reduced fatalities.

To further decrease the number of attacks the Australian Department of the Environment, Water, Heritage and the Arts offered the following handy list of precautions: Avoid swimming far from the shore, at the mouth of a river or on drop-offs to deeper water. Avoid swimming in dirty water, swimming alone or with domestic animals, near people fishing, or at dusk or night, and to leave the water immediately if schools of fish begin to behave erratically. So, basically, don't get in the water at all.

The exhibition also featured a skeleton of the jaws of another huge shark and Boz and I took photos of each other standing within them to give a gauge of the size. Weirdly, none of this put us off having a crack at surfing the next day. It should have, but it didn't.

In the end, we splashed around for about an hour, catching a grand total of no waves in choppy, small, onshore conditions. I have a photo of me standing on the beach at Surfers Paradise holding the surfboard and looking as cool as it was possible to look with stubbie shorts and a wispy 80s moustache. That alone was worth the surfboard rental fee.

These days, as a dedicated longboard surfer, I take the threat posed by the men in grey suits far more seriously. I lost a close friend to a shark attack and several other mates have had frighteningly close calls. Actually, sharks frighten the bejesus out of me, but they are part of the deal if you want to surf.

Recently, at Pakiri Beach North of Auckland, New Zealand, a friend and I were getting ready to ride the waves. It was a beautiful day and there was a solid two-foot swell running, perfect for the ten-foot boards we were planning to take out. As we were putting on our wetsuits, we noticed a rangy, super-fit guy also getting ready to go out. We said G'day and chatted about breaks we had recently surfed. He was in New Zealand on holiday, but his normal spot was Snapper Rock on the Gold Coast of Australia, a famous surf break that attracts the best surfers in the world.

He was in the process of putting on his wetsuit and, as he stripped off his T-shirt, my friend and I noticed a semi-circle of red marks that were scabbed over on his left forearm. My mate and I looked at each other nervously, then I asked the question on both our minds.

"Ahh, those marks on your arm, they're not umm..."

He cut me off with a dismissive wave.

"Shark bite, yeah mate, just a little one, but. He was only having a nibble."

We were stunned. Only an Aussie could be so casual about a shark attack. You really have to love the Australians.

The rest of Boz and my trip passed relatively uneventfully. I had survived my first Australian adventure and had a taste of overseas travel. Before our plane had touched down in New Zealand, I had decided that I wanted to see more of the world and began planning my big O.E. Overseas Experience, something that a lot of young Kiwis do.

I wanted to base myself in England and tour Europe, taking

Eula, my lovely girlfriend (who was to become my wife) with me. Well, not so much taking her with me. She was not the sort of girl to be led anywhere, but rather sharing the experience together.

She was just finishing her Master's degree in English at Massey University and I was working as a security guard, so we decided once we had the necessary funds I'd go to London and set up a base while she completed her study. Then she'd join me.

You'd think someone that smart would know better.

CHAPTER THREE

SNOW IN IRELAND

UK and Ireland circa 1985. I relied on the scribbles of Snow, my travelling companion. His diary is surprisingly detailed but not often in helpful ways. He talks a lot about Guinness.

Eula and I had been living in London for several years by now. I say living, but it was more existing, which is not a dig at the UK but merely a comment on our precarious financial position.

I had left New Zealand with very few skills unless you count failed policeman and unskilled ex-security guard. Most employers didn't. I had no trade and no university qualifications. My school results were average and, weirdly, the fact I'd gone to New Plymouth Boys High School held little sway in England. Eton, it was not.

I got work as a labourer, and a landscape gardener, but neither job paid well. Eula was doing slightly better. Her MA in English meant she was more employable, and she picked up a job for the London branch of the Bank of Scotland. The Scottish reputation for parsimony was well earned and there wasn't a lot left over from her monthly pay cheque. Fortunately, neither of us was used to having money, so we were able to live on a budget and were salting savings away.

A friend of ours, nicknamed Snow for his extremely blond hair —New Zealanders are a creative bunch—had expressed interest in a boy's trip and Eula had given me the nod to proceed (on a relatively small budget). Looking back, this was extremely generous of her. We were saving for a big trip around Europe and she could have fairly insisted that we kept all our money for that.

Throughout our shared life she always acknowledged and accommodated my need to go on boy's own adventures. These were trips that held little or no interest for her; a trek through some remote jungle was her idea of hell, but she never begrudged me this sort of travel. I tried to reciprocate with offers to pay for girls' trips with her friends, but she rarely took me up on these. She preferred spending time with her family.

Sharon, Snow's partner (a lovely Canadian), had also given the trip the green light and the initial plan for the boy's adventure was to go and see mountain gorillas in the jungles of Uganda. Our partners were dubious about the idea, given that Uganda had a habit of descending into chaos due to military coups and civil unrest. We also had no jungle experience, and I suspected that Snow's hair colour would make him extremely attractive to the gorillas. I posited that this could easily end up in an interspecies forced marriage and even though I had no basis whatsoever for my theory, but it was enough to put Snow off the trip.

We went to Ireland instead. That's pretty safe, right?

Not Belfast in 1985, it wasn't, but we excluded Northern Ireland from our itinerary when we told the girls. We were definitely going there, but didn't want them to worry. Given our combined history of trouble, it was a deception born of kindness.

To prepare for our adventure, Snow and I bought a tent and some camping equipment. We did zero research and didn't even think about the size or shape of the tent or what its comfort/weatherproof properties were. We just bought the cheapest one.

In writing, these last few sentences are called foreshadowing, which means setting up something that will come into effect later in the story. In this case, it could also be known as impending doom.

As a rule, basing your purchasing decision solely on price is not the wisest course of action, but financial constraints were in play, though with the benefit of hindsight, spending a few extra quid would have been a much smarter move.

You will have noticed there is a recurring theme to my misadventures. I barrel headfirst into situations woefully under-prepared and with little consideration or regard for consequences. It's not a strategy I'd recommend, but it makes life interesting.

Thus prepared, Snow and I set sail for Ireland, which isn't a figure of speech as we were too cheap to take a flight, and opted for the ferry instead. This meant catching a train from Euston Station in London to Holyhead in Wales—at least this is what we did according to Snow's diary of the trip, which he has forwarded to me as a memory jogging tool. This is a stroke of luck as my recollections are fractured at best, so some good news is there.

I don't remember Holyhead at all. I'm sure it's a very nice seaport town and my lack of recollection should not be seen as a reflection of the city or its environs, or maybe it should. You'd think I'd remember something, but let's be generous and put that down to a long train trip, three-hundred-and sixty-three kilometres and a journey time of over six hours.

After reading about Holyhead, I realised I missed out on the following attractions, of which only one actually attracts me.

Here's a fun game. Guess which one?

First, we have the Holyhead Maritime Museum, which is housed in what is claimed to be Wales's oldest lifeboat house (clue—it's not this one).

Then we have Penrhos Country Park, the number four thing to do in Holyhead, according to TripAdvisor.

Now, I was prepared to exclude this straight away until I saw a photo of the park. It didn't feature stunning scenic wetland vistas or a picturesque woodland walk. Oh no. The picture was of a cemetery.

The thing that struck me instantly was the names on the gravestones—Tiggy Puss, Dinkie, Whisky and Brandy.

I assumed these were traditional Welsh names and my mind wandered back to days of yore when Tiggy Puss, Whiskey and

Brandy would meet at the local tavern for a pint of braggot and a plate of leeks and chips. They'd moan about how Dinkie hogged the crempogs at the last Dawnsio gwerin (look it up) and then pop out for a bit of hedgelaying.

On closer inspection, I also spotted the names Sooty and Champ, and it dawned on me that this was a pet cemetery. I was strangely disappointed; I'd love to meet someone called Tiggy Puss.

Using a photo of a pet cemetery to advertise the park intrigued me, but not enough, so this also wasn't the attractive attraction.

No, the thing I was immediately drawn to was that Holyhead's cliffs were used for *coasteering*, which is a local water sport that involves jumping off cliffs at different heights.

They had me at 'jumping off cliffs.'

Sadly, I didn't learn any of this until later, which means the cliffs remain un-jumped off by myself and Snow.

According to his diary, while on the excruciatingly long train journey, we chatted to a few other low-budget travellers and received some interesting intel on must-see attractions in the Emerald Isles (pubs). We then boarded the ferry, had a pie and some sandwiches, watched Police Academy in the TV lounge and played Space Invaders.

I know what you are thinking. Here are two erudite, sophisticated travellers out to experience all the cultural and artistic wonders the world offers. That was us all right, exactly like James Bond, but not so much 007 but 010101. Licensed to kill .... Donkey Kong.

The other notable thing on the ferry ride was our first possible bomb incident. We were very much aware of the IRA's proclivity for blowing up anything to do with the UK. This was only a year after the infamous Brighton Hotel bombing.

On the 12th of October 1984, the Provisional Irish Republican Army launched an assassination attempt on British Prime Minister Margaret Thatcher. One of their members, Patrick Magee, planted a long-delay time bomb under the bath in his room at the Grand Hotel in Brighton. The Prime Minister and her Cabinet were staying at the hotel for the Conservative Party conference. The bomb detonated at approximately 2.54 am, and the blast brought down a five-ton chimney stack which crashed through the floors into the basement.

The PM narrowly escaped injury, with the explosion destroying her suite's bathroom but leaving the bedroom and sitting room untouched.

The bomb used in the attack contained twenty pounds of gelignite, which was described as a 'small bomb' by IRA standards. How comforting.

Five people were killed in the blast and thirty-four were injured, several very seriously. It was a brazen and brutal attack that brought 'the troubles' sharply into focus, even for a couple of Kiwi lads who had nothing to do with any of it.

It was against this background of escalating sectarian violence that we sailed towards Ireland. So, I was understandably nervous when a young bloke with a strong Irish accent asked me to mind his bag on the ferry while he went to the bathroom. Snow, in a heart-warming display of unity, immediately moved to the other side of the boat and mimed being blown up. Fortunately, the most dangerous thing in the guy's backpack was his laundry, and he returned from the toilet, thanked me and retrieved his property. If he was a terrorist, he was a very polite one. Snow came over, claimed to have had my back (despite overwhelming evidence to the contrary), and said he wasn't even remotely worried. I suspect this was a lie.

We arrived in Dublin late morning after a mercifully calm crossing. It was raining when we landed. This was to become a theme for the trip. We hadn't realised that Ireland can be a tad wet. We should have factored this into our tent buying (see foreshadowing) but hadn't.

Given that the weather was inclement, and we were exhausted from travelling, we treated ourselves to a room at a youth hostel. We were youths, after all. The accommodation would cost us a grand total of three pounds fifty each and even my budget could stretch to that. The bugger was we couldn't get into said rooms until after five that night, so that meant staggering around the slick streets of old Dublin town, killing time.

My impression of Dublin was definitely coloured by the weather, but also the time we were there. It was a time of high unemployment and economic stagnation. This meant there was a general feeling of dereliction and disillusionment on the streets. I remember homeless people and closed shops. To me, Dublin was a place we wanted to get out of very quickly and not a great introduction to Ireland. Of course, today it's a bustling cosmopolitan city, so don't let me put you off.

Snow and I also weren't the most culturally adventurous travellers. We could probably have gone to a museum or art gallery, and I might have these days, but back then it was straight to the amusement arcade and movie theatre to slaughter some invaders from space and take in another cinematic masterpiece—Porky's Revenge.

After that, we finally got into the hostel where we engaged with all the other lively young people and partied the night away—no wait, we didn't. We slept for twelve hours instead.

Our second day in Ireland was overcast, so a good one then.

We had decided pre-trip that our modes of transport were to be buses, trains and hitchhiking. This was back in the day when sticking your thumb out to cadge a lift was still a relatively safe and acceptable way to get around. We didn't even consider hiring a car—see budgetary restrictions. Anyway, as I said, we thought Dublin didn't have much to offer, having given it one wet afternoon, when we were tired, to prove itself.

Sorry Dublin, I know a lot of people love you, but we just didn't click. I returned to Ireland many years later with my wife and daughter, but again I have no memories of Dublin; I'm assuming we bypassed it. I have vague memories of a brewery, but honestly, this is Ireland, so that could be anywhere.

Leaving the capital behind, Snow and I set off for the picturesque village of Enniskerry.

According to the Wicklow tourist site, *Enniskerry features superb cafes and shops as well as a host of picture-postcard cottages and a charming village triangle. The clock tower in the centre of the village is also a very attractive feature*.

So, no amusement arcades then. What sort of place was this?

I do like a village triangle, though, so much better than boring old squares and quadrangles. What I'd really like to see is a village dodecahedron. This is probably the only shape I remember from high school mathematics because the word is fun to say.

However, this wasn't our destination of choice. Attractive clock or not, we were headed for Glendalough, 'the valley of the two lakes'. Our philosophy being why visit one lake when you can see two? That's just efficient.

I don't recall Snow or me doing a lot of pre-trip planning. I think we had a rough idea of where we wanted to go, but there was very little research done. We were playing it by ear instead. Unpredictability can be a harsh mistress and this methodology worked against us more often than not. In this instance, we got a little of both. We were able to hitch a ride in a van with a very nice guy who went out of his way to get us close to Glendalough, within a mile, but we failed to catch another lift and had to walk the rest of the way. We arrived mid-afternoon and went straight to the pub for a pint of Guinness. I don't particularly like the thick black beer. It tastes like soot (controversial), but when in Ireland...

After our obligatory pints, we left the pub to explore the Monastic City of Glendalough. It's one of the most important monastic sites in Ireland, not that this meant squat to Snow or me, as neither of us had a monastic bone in our bodies. I remember an impressive round tower. It was thirty metres high, built in the twelfth century and very, umm, round. We looked at this architectural marvel for about five minutes, then wandered off to find somewhere to pitch our tent.

Aside from its ecclesiastical magnificence, Glendalough is set in a lovely green valley surrounded by pine trees and farmland. We found a semi-flat stretch of paddock not far from town and asked the farmer if we could pitch our tent on his land. Somewhat surprisingly, he said yes, so that was us sorted for the night.

Actually, less sorted than we'd hoped because this is when we found out what a colossal mistake we'd made with our tent choice.

I'm a big guy. Six feet tall and solid with wide shoulders. Snow is shorter but equally stocky, factors we should have taken into account when perusing camping equipment. Our tent turned out to measure six by four, meaning we barely fit inside with our heads at one end and our feet nearly out of the flap.

We were also backpacking and hadn't taken our packs into consideration. They couldn't fit inside the tent, which meant leaving them at the door with the flap open—a shitty situation for security, warmth and weather tightness. Not that the tent makers had employed cutting-edge waterproofing technology in its construction. I don't even think it had a rain cover.

Once we'd realised the magnitude of our error, it was too late to do anything about it, so we took the only option open to us and went back to the pub. Once there, we played cards with the locals and downed three pints of Guinness each, calculating that this was the minimum amount required to give ourselves a fighting chance of getting some sleep.

According to Snow's diary, it didn't work, and I farted a lot.

I blamed the Guinness.

CHAPTER FOUR

TWO MEN AND A LEAKY TENT

Ireland circa 1985, in Glendalough. Snow's diaries continue to surprise, but not always in good ways.

Here's what we've established so far: My blond mate Snow and I are in Ireland; we are woefully under-prepared; our tent is ill-suited for purpose; We have little in the way of funds; Guinness tastes like soot.

To continue:

Weather: Overcast and cold. Just what you'd expect at what is laughingly called the height of summer. I've seen summers, and this wasn't one.

Snow's diary entries have turned out to be factual and humorous, but there isn't a lot of descriptive prose. Fortunately, we have me for that, and I'm embellishing the hell out of everything.

The dairy comes in handy for adding those little details that would have been long forgotten. This is particularly true concerning food. Snow meticulously categorised our meals and has provided a definitive answer to the question: why is my digestive system so messed up?

According to the book of Snow, we rose at 10 a.m., solidly embracing gentlemen's hours, and had a tin of fruit salad for breakfast.

A solid start to our five-plus a day. We then went into town, immediately found a tea shop and chowed down on cheese sandwiches and hot scones.

All very civilised and a far cry from the previous evening's dinner. It had been the meal that stands out for its unrelenting awfulness. And, I've eaten service station pies.

As you'll recall, we'd set up camp in a farmer's field quite far from town.

Snow and I had purchased some basic supplies the previous day, and we whipped up some baked beans and an omelette for dinner. Not exactly haute cuisine, but it doesn't sound too bad, does it?

Ha! You fools.

You haven't taken into account the fact that we bought our camp stove and other cooking equipment at the same place as the tent and with the same parsimonious intent. This meant our gas stove's temperature controls were so temperamental that it either spluttered off (normally without us noticing) or roared like a flamethrower. There was no in-between.

We had also only bought one pot.

Now you're getting a glimpse of how this meal is going to go. That's right, half-burnt, half-undercooked, lumpy omelette stewed in the same pot as either burning hot or stone-cold baked beans.

And this isn't the worst bit, nope.

There was one more ingredient to add to this congealed mess: midges, aka sandflies, aka swarming bitey bastards.

Little did we know Ireland was a haven for these extremely irritating flying legions of mini-vampires. Apparently, they love humid climates that lack bright sunshine—well-done Irish summer. You've done it again.

They also travel in swarms and come out in the evening, like, say, dinner time, when you're cooking outdoors in a farmer's field.

Fun fact. Only female midges bite, and only when they are pregnant for a second or third time.

Hey, I get it. Hubby midge is down the pub with the boys. He's not rubbing your back, your ankles are swollen, your hormones are all over the place, there's the pain of childbirth to worry about, none of your wardrobe fits, and then there's the financial pressure. I'd bite too.

And swarm they did—right over our campsite and into the omelette/baked bean slush. They landed on it, in it, and all over us as we tried to eat it.

I guess we could have tried to make the best of things, like classifying the midges as extra protein, and eaten with some degree of decorum. Instead, we ran around waving our arms in the air like inflatable air dancers at a car sales yard, and covering the field with splodges of midge filled eggs.

In our defence, it's disconcerting trying to eat a meal that's also trying to eat you.

A hell of a lot of them must have been pregnant; that's all I'm going to say.

Back to the present.

After our scones, we checked out a souvenir shop. We were certain the perfect gifts for the girls would be leprechauns and plastic four-leafed clovers. We were wrong.

Fortunately, Snow and I had the good sense not to buy anything, so we left the shop and made-our-way to the much-vaunted Glendalough double lakes.

Very nice they were, too.

We rambled along the pebbled shores, marvelled at the crystal-clear water and the bush-clad hills reflected in the lake's surface and carved ourselves some semi-genuine eighteenth-century Irish walking sticks.

I love a good walking stick and the ones we fashioned were pretty damned nice. Snow's carpentry skills really came to the fore. Maybe we could sell them to the souvenir shop, or at least trade them for leprechauns.

We paused in our tramp for a traditional Irish snack of ice cream and chips and then continued around the lake back to our starting point, where there was a convenient pub. Cue more Guinness and ham and cheese sandwiches.

Rambling is hungry work.

Whilst there, we played pool and chatted with some nice American girls. Once the pooling, Guinnessing, and chatting were done, we went back to the tent to get a torch. With light now in hand, we went to another pub where we played pool and chatted with some more Americans.

Looking back, it would have been easier to stay in the first pub, especially as the second pub inexplicably lost power, and we had to return to the tent.

Chatting to Americans, like rambling, is also hungry work, so Snow and I stopped at a restaurant on the way back.

It was closed. Somehow, we managed to buy a cold chicken for four pounds.

The travel diary doesn't reveal how this miracle happened, so I'm going to surmise we met a man in an alley selling cold chickens from inside his coat.

We ate our food then, and the miracles continue, received a lift back to our tent from the man who sold us the chicken. Maybe he was selling the chickens out of a van. That would make more sense.

You'd think enough had happened that day, but you'd be wrong.

It took a while to get settled into our respective sleeping bags; given that the flap was open and my feet were sticking out, comfort was not easily attained.

There were more accusations of excessive flatulence from Snow, which I vehemently denied. Actually, I laughed and did it again, but let's not go into that.

Sometime after midnight, we settled, and sleep crept up on us.

The night sky was pitch black: a gentle breeze whispered through the trees; the midges had gone; the chicken was digesting; the farting had stopped, and our sleeping bags cocooned us in a nest of warmth and comfort.

We were at peace with the world.

All was well.

Until... a sudden, piercing, bone-curdling shriek rent the air just outside our tent. This was followed by the sound of something crashing through the undergrowth.

I snapped awake but lay rooted to the spot in terror. I looked over at Snow; his eyes were wide, and panic painted his face.

"What the hell was that?" I hissed.

"Sounded like a scream." He said helpfully.

"Go out and have a look."

"I'm not going out there. You go."

There was no way in hell I was leaving the tent, and I said so.

"So, what are we going to do," enquired Snow, "lie here and get murdered in our sleep?"

"I think we'll be safe if we stay in the tent," I said, with absolutely no reason to believe this was true.

Snow nodded. We lay quietly for a few minutes.

"It could have been a Banshee," ventured Snow. "They're Irish, aren't they?"

He may have been onto something. The scream was certainly Banshee-like. All I knew about them was that they flew around in raggedy white cloaks, were terrifying, and their cry signified an imminent death. This was obviously less than ideal.

"It didn't sound human, did it?"

Snow shook his head.

We should have stopped this line of thinking immediately, given that Banshees were mythical and we were two rational adults. This theory was, however, better than the alternative—that someone had come to actual physical harm outside our tent.

I was worried. If there had been an assault, a murder, or attempted murder, we should probably get up and try to help. This would, of course, expose us to the murderer, which had little to recommend it.

There were a few more awkward moments of silence, and then Snow spoke. "I think I heard someone running away after the scream."

"Yeah, I heard that too."

"So, it was probably just kids playing a prank," he continued hopefully.

This was by far the best scenario, so I latched onto it.

"Yeah, that'll be it."

I'm not sure either of us believed this, but pretending we did was infinitely preferable to getting up and having a look. Besides, it was cold outside.

We tried to settle down, but were too anxious to get a good night's rest.

Sleep didn't come until the early hours-of-the-morning and, when it did, it was fitful. I could tell by Snow's bleary-eyed appearance that his repose had been similar to mine. We were reluctant to leave the tent, even in the comforting light of day, fearing what we might find.

The answer was nothing. Our view was pastoral perfection. Well, not quite. Naturally the day was overcast, and the midges were back, but aside from that, we could hear birds twittering in the trees, sheep were doing sheep things nearby, and the day radiated country calm. There was nothing to show that carnage had occurred anywhere near our tent.

We packed up our gear and headed for town. On the way, we stopped to thank the farmer for the (terrifying) use of his paddock. His wife was the only one home; he must have been out tilling, ploughing, reaping, or whatever it is farmers do.

We thought it was our duty to warn this lovely, generous woman of the potentially lethal maniac stalking their fields. The farmer's wife laughed. Not the reaction we had been expecting.

What we heard was the sound of a hawk hunting. She said their cry can be harrowing if you didn't know what it was. No kidding. I'm not sure why hawks bother having razor-sharp talons. They could just scare their prey to death.

After our usual healthy breakfast of tea, scones and sandwiches, we sallied forth to see how far the generous people of Ireland were prepared to transport us for free.

As we would most likely travel in personal vehicles, we decided our semi-genuine eighteenth-century Irish walking sticks would have to be left behind. It was a sad moment. They had been loyal companions.

We started with a half-hour walk to Laragh, stopped at the pub for a pre-hitchhiking pint, and then set our thumbs to work. Our goal was Wexford, and we had the rest of the day to get there.

The first people to pick us up were two young Irish guys in a sixteen-seater van. I'm not sure why they had a commercial vehicle. There was no sign-writing on the side, and I didn't ask. They took us to Arklow and picked up three French hitchhikers and one Irish girl. Maybe they were starting a traveller's ride-sharing business, but that didn't make sense, given that the whole point of hitchhiking was to avoid paying for your trip. Perhaps they were just nice guys who liked driving vans; we'll never know.

Once in Arklow, we ignored whatever sights were available, and played snooker instead. Snow and I were keen pool and snooker players. I can hold my own with most sports and activities, and it's the same on the green felt. If my eye is in, I can be quite good, even capable of a few trick shots, but it depends on the day.

I have my misspent youth to thank, having spent many free (and not so free) school periods at the pool hall. I would generally bunk out of physics or maths classes, justifying my absence by claiming I was getting real-world experience in calculus, trajectory, friction and force by attempting to double the black off the left-hand cushion into the corner pocket. None of the teachers bought this explanation, which only confirmed my suspicion that school had no practical use. Detention for Glenn.

After our snooker game, I made a disturbing discovery. I had left my sleeping bag in the back of the van. This was a disaster of epic proportions. Of all the equipment to lose, this was the worst. It was a really good sleeping bag I bought in New Zealand, especially for my overseas travel. It was expensive, very well made and warm to minus ten degrees, which, I reasoned, would be great for all the polar exploration I was going to do (none). It was equally handy for winter in the UK, which we can all agree is akin to arctic conditions.

Losing my sleeping bag would also put a serious dent in my travelling money as I would have to buy a new one and they are not cheap.

We rushed out of the pub and hunted for any sign of the sixteen-seater. The chance that the two guys would still be in town was low, but we were in luck. The van was parked close to where we'd been dropped off as the men had had lunch in town. They turned up several minutes later saying they hardly ever ate here, so we were really fortunate. Disaster averted. For once, good fortune had cupped my testicles with warm hands. It wouldn't last.

We hit the road again and got a lift from Arklow to Gorey, still en route to Wexford. We became marooned in Gorey, which sounds like the beginning of a great country and western song:

Battened down in Baton Rouge and gummed up in Gorey, I lost my heart to a girl called Tiggy Puss, but that's another story.

I have no memory of Gorey, and, looking at it on a map, I can see why. It's one of those towns similar to thousands worldwide whose sole purpose seems to be for people to pass through or get stuck in.

We stood roadside for an hour, our thumbs extended hopefully to the side, smiles plastered on our faces, trying not to look like psychopaths.

Just as we were about to give up, a lady in a tired Mazda slid to a stop before us. It was the type of car a used car salesman would advertise as having one careful lady owner. I can tell you from experience that this particular lady owner was anything but careful. She drove like a lunatic on the run from an asylum. She was the sort of driver who chatted continuously, keeping her attention on her passengers rather than on the road. This made for a white knuckle ride, but one we were grateful for because she went out of her way and took us straight to the Wexford campground. Success.

We made it with only minor trouser staining.

Ducking under a spray of flying gravel, we waved goodbye to our saviour and watched as she roared away; the Mazda screaming to be let out of second gear.

We were stoked that we had arrived not only in one piece, but had also been deposited right at the door of our destination. We went into the office and paid for our tent site. We planned to pitch the tent, and go into town while there was still daylight. This was easier said than done. Sadly, we had learned nothing from our close call with the sleeping bag and had ratcheted things up a notch by leaving all of our tent poles in the lady's Mazda. There was no way we'd catch her; the way she drove, she was probably several counties away.

Here's a riddle for you. What do you call a tent without poles?

Answer: Absolutely useless.

We looked at the pile of canvas on the ground, now as functional as a bouncy castle shot by a harpoon, and wondered what to do next.

There was only one answer. We had to splash out and get a room in a bed & breakfast. This extravagance cost us eight pounds fifty each. That's two cold chickens!

Once we'd booked our rooms, we went to the pub to drown our sorrows and curse our carelessness. Then it was back to the B&B for a hot shower. Why? Because it was raining.

Of course it was.

CHAPTER FIVE

GO ANY FURTHER DOWN THAT ROAD AND YOU'RE DEAD

Northern Ireland, 1985- The book of Snow skips forward a few chapters here. Still plenty of great craic though, as they say in the Emerald Isles, which, ironically, this chapter isn't really about.

Weather: Overcast.

I'm going to save the rest of our travels in central Ireland for another day and go straight to Northern Ireland now.

I told you I was going to mess with timelines. You can't say you weren't warned (unless you didn't read the intro).

After several weeks of hard and wet travelling, Snow and I hitch-hiked our way toward the northern part of the country.

Our extended thumbs paid dividends six kilometres south of the border when we were picked up by three young guys in an old van.

They were headed to Belfast through Dundalk and said they'd take us all the way to the city. We crossed the border at about three pm and were astounded there were no control points or customs to go through. The only way we knew we'd left Southern Ireland behind was because we'd driven past a large hill with a stone fence through the middle of it. We were told one side was Northern

Ireland and the other Southern. The lack of border controls was weird, especially as we had heard about the incredibly stringent security between the divided countries.

We didn't have to wait long before we saw first-hand evidence of the troubles. The reality of the situation hit hard as we travelled through Newry and saw the aftermath of the devastation that had been wrought on the police station six months earlier.

On the 28th of February 1985, the Provisional Irish Republican Army (IRA) launched a heavy mortar attack on the Royal Ulster Constabulary (RUC) base in Newry. The homemade mortar launcher was bolted onto the back of a stolen Ford lorry. Shortly after 6.30 pm, nine shells were launched from the truck, which was parked about two-hundred-and-thirty metres from the base.

At least one twenty-three-kilogram shell landed on a portacabin containing a canteen where many officers were having their evening tea break. Nine police officers were killed and thirty-seven people were injured, including twenty-five civilian police employees.

Another shell hit the observation tower, and the rest landed inside and outside the perimeter of the base. It was the highest death toll inflicted on the RUC in its entire history.

After the attack, the British government launched a multi-million-pound program of construction to protect bases from similar attacks. The Newry base had been rebuilt and reinforced, though there was still evidence of scorch marks on the exterior walls. High, blast-proof barriers had been built, and the building bristled with barbed wire and heavily armed soldiers. Armoured police vehicles sat at the entrance to the station. Tensions were obviously still high, and it was a sobering sight.

At the time, the New Zealand police were unarmed. Access to firearms was available, if necessary, though this seldom happened and was rarely seen by members of the public. As a former member of the constabulary, I was fairly comfortable with guns, having been armed myself on several occasions, but I wasn't used to seeing military hardware readily on display like it was here. To Snow, it was something else entirely. He could barely believe what he was seeing. Our naivety and slack-jawed curiosity brought about our first armed confrontation.

Not long after passing the police station, a heavily armed military vehicle (a Humber Pig) pulled onto the road directly in front of the van. There was a manned machine gun on the roof and Snow and I gawped at the vehicle in astonishment.

The Irish guys in the car saw what we were doing and hissed at us.

"For fuck's sake, don't stare at them. They'll think we're up to something."

Too late. The soldier on the roof swung the gun towards us and the vehicle flashed its lights, indicating we should pull over.

Our driver did as he was told, not that he had a lot of option. His mates issued hushed instructions. We were told to sit very still, make no sudden moves, and avoid eye contact.

The soldiers in the back of the armoured truck leapt from the vehicle and fanned out on either side of the van. The one who moved to our side carried a large Armalite AR15 self-loading rifle and the barrel was pointed directly at us. I couldn't help but notice he had his finger curled around the trigger.

It was an incredibly tense moment.

The driver very, very slowly wound down the window and explained to the soldiers that we were harmless tourists from New Zealand and unused to seeing armed soldiers.

I was going to add that we weren't worth shooting as the paperwork would have been horrendous, but thought better of it. I don't think levity would have been appreciated.

The lead soldier asked a few more questions, took a long, slow look at us (which I swear lasted about three years) then gave a curt nod and motioned for the other soldiers to return to the vehicle. They backed off, but kept their weapons levelled at us the entire time.

After the armoured truck had driven away, the driver let out a huge sigh of relief.

"Fook me," he said to his mates. "That's the last time I pick up hitchhikers from New Zealand."

'Dammit,' I thought, 'we've ruined it for all Kiwis... again.'

Snow and I mumbled apologies, but there was no need. The

mood inside the van was jovial now that we hadn't been riddled with bullets.

As we neared Belfast the fortifications, checkpoints and presence of armed soldiers grew. I was surprised the Irish guys had been so tense when we were pulled over and asked if they were used to being stopped and searched. They said they were, but added that if they hadn't stopped, the soldiers would have opened fire on the van. I guess you can never really get used to some things and having a soldier level a gun at you is close to the top of the list.

Our driver dropped us off in the central city. The rain was heaving down, but that was the least of our concerns. The boarded-up buildings and roving groups of armed soldiers brought home the seriousness of the situation we'd stumbled blindly into. I'd like to say we found a B&B and settled in for the evening to contemplate the difficult political and social situation that had been forced upon this profoundly divided country, but we didn't. We went to the pub.

As we returned to our B&B later that night, we stopped to watch one of the army patrols. There were six soldiers in the unit and as they walked cautiously through the streets, in a staggered formation, the last soldier in line would slowly turn around, making sure no one was coming up behind them. They were incredibly well-drilled and extremely vigilant. I guess their lives depended on it.

They had clocked us very early on and quickly ascertained we were no threat. We made sure not to watch too closely as we knew our status could rapidly change and these boys were not messing around.

The following day (raining) we met up with an Aussie guy called Kevin. He was also hitchhiking around Ireland and told us there was a march planned in town to celebrate the tenth anniversary of Internment. It had been introduced by the Unionist government in 1971 and ended in 1975.

Operation Demetrius, as it was called, involved mass British army arrests and internment without trial of over three-hundred-and-forty people from Catholic and nationalist backgrounds.

This was designed to smash the IRA, but the intelligence was poor and scores of the people detained had no connection with the organisation. Naturally, the Unionists supported the move, but it prompted serious violence from Nationalists and served as a recruitment boon for the IRA. During the length of the operation, almost two thousand people were interred and the annual commemorations regularly led to unrest.

Obviously deaf to the political sensitivity of the day and unaccountably unconcerned about very real threats to life and limb, Snow and I thought we'd join the March because we might see some 'cool rioting'.

Apparently, this was my idea, and it's up there with the worst I've ever had. And that's saying something.

Kevin was clearly cut from the same cloth and said he'd tag along. With this stupid purpose in mind, we donned our packs and wandered blindly through the streets of Belfast. We ambled along, headed roughly to where we thought the centre of the city might be, when suddenly a massive armoured Land Rover swerved off the road, mounted the curb directly in front of us and shuddered to a stop, blocking our way.

An agitated RUC cop wrenched open his door and yelled at us. "What the hell are you three playing at? Do you have a death wish?"

Snow, Kev and I were very confused. We assured him we didn't.

"Then why the hell are you walking towards Falls Road (an IRA stronghold) with union jacks on your back?"

Oh Shit. The penny dropped. Snow and I were patriotic Kiwis and had sewn the New Zealand flag onto the back of our packs. It hadn't occurred to us that our flag contained the union jack, the hated symbol of British oppression for the Irish Nationalists. Kevin was flagless, but that wouldn't have saved him.

We explained the situation to the cop, and he immediately calmed down. Several other RUC policemen exited the vehicle and began scanning the streets to make sure no one had clocked the dumb Antipodeans.

"Honestly," he said with a shake of the head, "go any further down that road and you're dead."

We apologised profusely for our ignorance and told him of our plans to see the march. This was met with more head shaking and we were advised in the strongest possible terms to steer clear of the area.

We agreed to stay away, and I started chatting with the cop about what it was like being a policeman in Northern Ireland, explaining that I'd recently been in the New Zealand Police. This broke the ice, and we immediately became kindred spirits. He wasn't much older than me and, even as an ex-cop, I still belonged to a universal brotherhood of law enforcement officers. It's the kind of job where shared adversity forms bonds. Quite often, cops don't have many friends outside the police and we band together.

"Do you really want to know what it's like being a cop in Belfast?" he asked.

I assured him I did. He gave me a grin and patted the bonnet of the truck. "Hop in the back then and we'll give you a tour of the city."

Snow, Kev and I couldn't believe our luck and jumped at the chance. Cruising Belfast with an armed RUC patrol—this was even cooler than seeing rioting!

We climbed into the back of the vehicle and sat on bench seats with three other RUC guys. The rear cabin was reinforced with heavily armoured panels and was windowless but had slits you could open to look out (or fire out) of. The officers were armed with Ruger .357 magnum pistols and one cradled a Heckler & Koch MP5 sub-machine gun on his knee.

As we drove through Shankill Road, one of the key loyalist areas, we were struck by the patriotism on display. Paving stones were covered with union jacks, British-style bunting hung from the houses and anti-IRA graffiti covered the walls.

Surprising close by were Falls Road and the Catholic areas which were similarly passionate with their loyalty to the cause. The graffiti here was pro-IRA, and spectacular murals were painted on the walls.

It was a very dangerous place for a URC patrol to be and as we got deeper into the militant areas; we were told to shut the viewing slots as there was a good chance someone would try to snipe through the openings.

The cops in the back told us horror stories that had become a daily reality during the troubles. They said the IRA had developed a bullet that could penetrate the armour on vehicles like the one we rode in but didn't have enough power to exit the other side. This meant the round bounced around inside until it hit something soft, like umm a police officer. Damn!

I remember one of the guys talking about a mate who, just weeks earlier, had his legs blown off by an improvised bomb. Hearing such personal reports brought home the very real danger we were in and I, for one, was thankful that our own countries had never experienced violence of this level.

Fortunately, we emerged from the most dangerous regions without anyone taking a pot-shot at us and were driven to a prosperous area overlooking the town. It was safe to leave the armoured truck here, and I was pleased to get into the fresh (though rainy) air.

I'm not claustrophobic, but the atmosphere in the rear of the vehicle was thick and heavy, especially when going through the troubled areas. It was a different story where the city's professional elite lived. Here the cops pointed out the lack of political or religious divide—Catholic houses sat alongside Protestant and there were no graffiti-covered walls or barricades.

It seemed the fighting was being done in working-class and slum areas. I'm not qualified or knowledgeable enough to comment on the complexities of the socio-political situation in Ireland, or indeed anywhere, but the difference between the rich and poor areas was stark and shocking.

Once outside the vehicle, I noticed it had a reinforced mesh scoop extending from the front bumper and I asked the driver about it. He said the weakest part of the armour on the vehicle was underneath and the IRA had worked out that if they rolled a beer keg under the front, then the vehicle would rise and become stranded, exposing the floor. A bomb could then be lobbed underneath. The mesh deflected the barrels.

Ye Gods, we were a long way from home.

At that moment, the patrol unit was called away to attend to a report of a group of suspicious youths gathering near the march. We were dropped back in town, managed some rushed thanks and goodbyes, and the armoured Land Rover sped away.

We'd spent almost two hours with the patrol, and I'm certain our tour wasn't even remotely sanctioned. It was a hell of an eye-opener with Kevin, Snow and me, deciding it would be a good idea not to linger in Belfast.

We grabbed a burger to celebrate still being alive and then booked a train to Portrush, a small seaside town on the north coast, where we were assured that we were less likely to die.

Belfast wasn't finished with us yet, though.

We had four hours to kill before our train left, more than enough time to get into further trouble. Rather than wandering around what was clearly a dangerous city, Snow and I went into a protestant area and play snooker.

We stowed our packs at the train station and wandered off. Even in the British zone, we didn't feel very safe, so we stuck to the snooker hall and headed back to the train station long before we were due to leave.

As we were returning, we passed close to a Catholic area and were alarmed to see several young guys heading our way. As soon as they saw us, they swung into action. Without a word, they bent over and grabbed rocks from the side of the road and began hurling them at us. They didn't even know who we were!

With large stones whizzing past our ears, Snow and I decided not to stick around to correct their mistake. We ran like hell. Fortunately, their aim was clouded by a rage we couldn't fathom and we got away, scared but undamaged.

Once we arrived at the relative safety of the train station, we stayed put. We'd had more than enough excitement for one day.

On the way to Portrush, we had a long chat with an Irish passenger who told us that train travel wasn't very safe at the moment. Just two days previously, the INLA (Irish National Liberation Army, a splinter group of the IRA) had bombed four carriages of a train travelling from Dublin to Belfast and had vowed to carry out more attacks.

Splendid. I wondered if it was too late to head to Uganda.

Luckily our train was bomb-free, and we arrived in Portrush at 8.30 pm. We were surprised to see Kevin the Aussie waiting for us at the train station. He had hitchhiked and had easily beaten us to the city.

We pitched our tent in some nearby sand dunes—a surface well known as camper friendly—then cruised into town for obligatory arcade games and food. We returned to the sand dunes just after midnight and stumbled around for ages trying to find our tent. The search was made more difficult because neither of us had a torch. It seems we weren't ready to join the SAS just yet. To make matters worse, our air mattresses had holes in them and our night's sleep was poor at best.

We woke to discover a large glowing ball in the sky. Rays of bright yellow light lit up the dunes. We stared in wonder. What was this strange phenomenon? After weeks of inclement weather, distant memories awoke deep within us. It was the sun! Oh My God, it was a fine day. Hallelujah. At last.

Kevin was richer than us, or me anyway, and had spent the night on an un-deflated mattress in a nearby bed & breakfast. He looked annoyingly refreshed and jauntily suggested we head to the harbour and organise a fishing trip. This was duly scheduled for 6.30 pm that evening and we spent the day visiting Giant's Causeway, a geological tourist attraction and much touted eighth wonder of the world, about 12 kilometres from Portrush.

I'm suspicious about eighth wonders—in fact, I'm pretty dubious about the seven wonders as well. The original seven—Pyramids of Giza, Colossus of Rhodes, Hanging Gardens of Babylon, Lighthouse of Alexandria, Mausoleum at Halicarnassus, Statue of Zeus at Olympia and Temple of Artemis at Ephesus—are rubbish, in my not so humble opinion. Only one survived, so they can't have been that wonderful, can they?

The new seven—The Great Wall of China, Petra, Christ the Redeemer, Machu Picchu, Chichen Itza, Colosseum and the Taj Mahal—are a bit better. At least you can see them. Not that I have, next book maybe.

As for the eighth wonder, every man and his dog claims one–Cambodia has Angkor Wat, Indonesia thinks Borobudur should be included, Sri Lanka claims Sigiriya, China heavily promotes the Terracotta Army, Canada thinks Niagara Falls, and someone even suggested the internet! New Zealand has claimed two, the pink and white terraces and Milford Sound. I went to Milford Sound recently. It was okay, but not the stuff of 'wonders'.

All we knew about Giant's Causeway was that it had a cool name and was made up of rocks. Since the last stones we saw were thrown at us, we thought it would be a nice change to see some that weren't, we hoped. And it was.

The causeway contains about forty thousand interlocking basalt columns and is a world heritage site. The tops of the columns form stepping stones that lead from the cliffs to under the sea. Most of the columns are hexagonal and look a bit like crazy paving or a game board for, you guessed it, giants. It definitely elicited some wonder from us, and we happily clambered around the rocks for several hours. Then suddenly, just to make sure we weren't getting too cocky weather-wise, it poured with rain for half an hour and we got absolutely soaked.

We slopped back to the bus and Snow announced he was going to stay in the same B&B as Kevin for the night. He'd had enough of being cold and wet and sleeping on a deflated mattress in a tent that was too small for us. What a wuss. I bravely announced that I would persist with camping, mainly because I was almost out of money. When we got back, I borrowed Kevin's shower. Not while he was in it. We'd become good mates, but not that good.

Once we'd all dried off, we headed to the wharf for our fishing trip. We were targeting that world-renowned game fish—mackerel.

Mighty mackerel, like the majestic marlin, but a lot smaller and not quite as fighty. Still, they both start with an M.

We had a great time. A lot of Blarney was talked and fish were caught. Our totals were Snow, fish leader with eighteen mackerel, Kingfish Kevin close behind with sixteen and me, slightly lagging with, umm, five. The absolute best part was returning to port, going to the Harbor Inn, and selling our fish for three pints of Guinness. Everyone won (except thirty-nine mackerel).

Over our hard-earned pints, we talked crap into the night. Kev had some excellent travelling horror stories. Terrifying tales of innocent tourists being brutally murdered and stuck into barrels of acid, a lot of them taken from remote campsites, it seemed. And with that, they said goodnight and prepared to go back to their comfy B&B while I wandered alone in the inky blackness, without a torch, through the isolated sand dunes in the dead of night. Possibly with psychotic murderers hunting nearby. I paused for about a millisecond and decided I didn't care what it cost, but I was joining them in the B&B. A good decision, as I wasn't butchered and put in an acid bath.

The next day, I checked my bank balance and discovered that I really had run out of money. It was time for me to pack up the tent and take the bus back to Dublin. I planned to avoid trains due to the threat of explosions (the main station in Belfast was bombed several weeks later), then ferry back to the UK. Snow was going to stay on a few more days and hitch back by himself.

And so we parted. We'd been through a lot together; countless hours on the road, sleeping side by side in a micro-tent, enjoying many a cold beer and hot pie.

Troubles, we'd seen a few, but not so many as Northern Ireland.

We had faced driving sleet, howling winds, constant rain, armed soldiers, stone-throwing youths, and much more with a sense of adventure and good humour (mostly).

It wasn't the most comfortable trip I've ever had, but it was certainly one of the most memorable. The outlook for the rest of Snow's trip?

Overcast with a high chance of rain.

CHAPTER SIX

BALI HI

Indonesia late 80s (with a quick detour to Norfolk Island). The only written evidence of these trips were a few jotted notes on an old A4 pad. I'd clearly meant to write a travel article about my adventures but hadn't gotten around to it. I discovered the notes under a pile of papers in my office drawer. I really must have a cleanout.

Let's leave rainy old Ireland behind and get a bit of Vitamin D on the sunny shores of Bali.

Ahh, Bali, a province of Indonesia and the westernmost of the Lesser Sunda Islands. Not that there is much 'Lesser' about the island; it's a morer place. More sun, more surf, more food, more alcohol, more fun for a lesser price.

This is well before the hordes of drunk Australians descended, before the Bali Bombing, before the high-rises and overpriced surf schools. This was before Kuta even had paved streets.

It was just the second overseas trip my lovely wife and I took as a married couple. The first was a somewhat disastrous honeymoon. Eula's parents had generously offered to pay for our postnuptial travel, as they knew we had no money. This was true. When we got married, we were both unemployed and had seven-hundred dollars in the bank.

They gave us two options, Sydney or Norfolk Island.

We knew nothing about Norfolk Island. I didn't even know it existed. Eula's knowledge was similar. We discovered it was a small Pacific Island between New Zealand and New Caledonia, so pretty much in the middle of nowhere.

It was a sovereign state of Australia and was settled by Great Britain in 1788 when the poms were grabbing anything they could in the South Pacific. True to form, they designated it a convict penal settlement, and it served as such from 6 March 1788 until the 5th of May 1855, except for an eleven-year hiatus from 1814 to 1825 where it lay abandoned—frankly, that's how they should have left it. Not that I'm bitter.

We picked Norfolk Island over Sydney because we thought we'd spend less money there. This assumption proved correct because there was absolutely nothing to spend it on.

The island was incredibly remote and the accommodation very basic. To cap things off, Eula got sick, and the only entertainment on offer was watching videotaped movies in our room. They had a grand total of four, and all of them were crap. The weather was rubbish, and I spent most of my time wandering around taking pictures of cows.

I mean, honestly, the thing the island is most known for these days is pine trees and having the largest population of tiger sharks in the world. Terrific. All sharks are bastards, but tiger sharks are the bastards the other bastards are scared of. They're incredibly aggressive and are quite happy to attack humans. No popping down to the beach for a quick swim, then—not unless you fancied coming back without a limb.

My most vivid memory of the trip was the evening the island held a convict-themed dinner and dance for all the poor sods who'd been suckered into honeymooning there. We were made to dress up in convict outfits, complete with cartoonish black arrows, and I have vague memories of sitting on the floor involved in some sort of forced-fun drinking game.

To her credit, Eula, who hated group activities, joined in and was a very good sport. She looked quite stunning in her convict costume, not a fetish I'd considered before, but hey, we were on our honeymoon. In the end, it wasn't the most memorable or romantic holiday we ever had, but at least we were together and could laugh about it later. Quite a bit later.

We were and remain grateful to her parents, because without them we wouldn't have had a honeymoon at all.

We were back in Bali, which we viewed as a much-needed romantic escape. We'd been married for a few years by then and both had steady, high-pressure jobs. She was making her way up the ladder of Farmer's Trading Company, the largest department store chain in New Zealand, and ironically, nothing to do with actual farming.

I was employed as a junior copywriter. I hadn't broken into the advertising industry yet, but was working for a newspaper and trying to impress.

We were both earning reasonable money, not large salaries by any means, but enough for a cheap holiday. Bali ticked that box and we stayed in Kuta on the coast for a few days and then go inland to Ubud. This was prior to me discovering surfing, so I wasn't worried about the quality of the waves. All we wanted was a relaxing holiday.

The hotel looked much flasher in the brochure, as they always do, but it was perfectly adequate and even had an in-room lizard, which I'll call Kevin. He was a small greenish-yellow chap with bulbous, darting eyes and weird feet. He (I say he, but I didn't actually check) was also disconcertingly stealthy. You'd look away for a few seconds and when you looked back, he'd be a metre closer. Spooky. I'm not normally great with critters, especially insects, but I don't mind reptiles, and Kevin was okay. I was sure he wouldn't hurt us or crawl over us in our sleep, so we were happy to share the room with him.

The local hawkers were more annoying. Whenever we ventured out of the hotel, we were greeted by cries of "Plait your hair" or "Watch for you, genuine Rolex".

Let's take that one at a time.

Neither my wife nor I wanted our hair plaited, and we said so, but this didn't stop the same question being asked by the same people multiple times each day. As our refusal was generally greeted with a good-natured smile and a nod, we didn't mind too much. They were just trying to get by. I don't understand why you'd even want a holiday hair plait, but I saw quite a few young women who had taken advantage of the offer, so what do I know?

The watch sellers were more persistent and therefore more aggravating. They seldom took no for an answer, and when I suggested they were playing fast and loose with the term 'genuine', they seemed to take it as a personal affront. We all knew the watches were fake, let's be clear on that, but the sellers seemed more determined to convince their customers the merchandise was real than to actually sell it. Certificates of authenticity were produced.

One even had 'authenticity' spelled wrong. How I laughed.

Stories of relations working in the factory were spun and the best trick of all, they'd admit that the watches before you were fake, and follow up with an offer to take you to a shop where the genuine ones were. Yeah, right? Last shower—me—no.

This was all part of the rich tapestry of Bali, that and stray dogs, scooters, street food, the smell of open drains, intricate wood carvings, incense, offerings to the many and various gods, temples, statues and of course beautiful beaches.

There was an unmistakable holiday vibe and to add to our good mood, we'd just changed some New Zealand currency and received about 17 billion Balinese Rupiah in return. Okay, I exaggerate, it was 16.5 billion.

We felt like Hollywood celebrities without the Botox or bodyguards.

I took a photo of Eula, lying on the bed in our hotel room surrounded by cash, which we decided was much better than the usual situation of being surrounded by bills.

The trip to Bali also marked a slow but steady widening of my culinary horizons. In my early years, I wasn't so much a meat and two veg guy, a more two meat and no veg bloke. My diet was little short of appalling (boy am I paying for it now) and I looked at any food other than bog-standard British with overt suspicion. However, when you're in Indonesia, you don't have much option but to eat Indonesian food, or just food as they call it.

Even though my dietary choices weren't great, I've never been into the fast-food chains, so it was eat local or nothing. Much to my surprise, it was pretty bloody good. Rome wasn't built in a day and neither was my tolerance for spice and heat, but progress was being made and I could soon order a Nasi Goerang with only a small amount of trepidation.

Eula had a much more refined palate than me (let's be honest, she had a much more refined everything than me) and was in her element, ordering things I gazed upon with mistrust, even one dish where the main protein looked suspiciously like a cousin of Kevin's.

The cocktails were also great. Exotic enough to be different, cheap enough for us to be experimental and alcoholic enough to expunge the worry about whether the ice was going to poison you. I have fond memories of one bar producing a cocktail for Eula and me that was housed inside a big, green coconut. Eye holes had been cut out and the whole drink looked like it was smiling. We certainly were after a few of them.

I can't remember what the cocktail was called, so I'm naming it Smiley Coconuthead. If you make one and want to use the name, royalties can be sent to my publisher.

Walking home from the bar that night, I had the crap scared out of me.

Eula and I were strolling along the dirt streets when suddenly a crazy-eyed figure leapt out at us. Thinking we were being attacked, I immediately snapped into a fighting pose, or I failed to react in any effective way. I can't remember which so let's not dwell on it.

Anyway, my bedraggled assailant yelled out "Gonzo" which struck me as odd as that was my nickname. How did this deranged creature know who I was? I had no friends in this part of the world, or so I thought. He turned out to be a mate of mine from my formative years in New Plymouth.

His name was Nigel, and he'd been travelling in Indonesia for several years. So long that he'd gone native. I remember watching him as he spoke, and he squatted down on his haunches as the Balinese did. He also ate rice with his hands. His hair was long and wild and he had a scraggly goatee. His skin was so darkly tanned that it was hard to tell he was European.

He and another friend were working for an oil exploration company and their jobs entailed them being dropped off at remote islands throughout the Pacific, acting as surveyors and advanced scouts. The stories he told were incredible, and worthy of their own book. He's an aspiring writer, so I'd better not steal his thunder and tell them.

It didn't surprise me he'd had such insane adventures. Nige is one of those slightly mad guys that live life at one-hundred-miles-an-hour. He is destined to either die in a spectacular car, boat, monkey, motorbike, alligator, Swedish twins, spa pool accident or outlive us all. At the moment, it's the latter but could still go either way. It was a pleasant and unexpected end to the evening.

The following day, we had a go at paragliding. Eula had wisely banned me from parachute jumping years earlier, convinced that some life-ending disaster would occur. I disagreed, saying that I'd be fine, and she was being paranoid. Given that she had never stopped me from doing anything else, I acquiesced and, to this day, have never leapt from a plane. On this occasion, she relented and agree that if the parachute was moored to a boat, then not much could go wrong.

She was half-right.

Initially, the flight was great with an exhilarating take off from the beach and a real sensation of speed and height hanging behind the boat as the parachute soared over the ocean.

However—with me, there's always a however—I hadn't listened to the instructions properly and had grabbed the wrong straps to hold on to.

I'd like to put this down to the poor English of the instructor, but it's more likely I was impatient to get going and wasn't listening. The result of my incorrect grip was two-fold. First, my arms were being forced backwards and my shoulders were getting very sore. Second, I was affecting the operation of the chute, which meant I was coming back into the landing zone on the beach with a lot more speed than normal.

The usual landing procedure entailed the boat cutting the

engine and the person in the parachute gently floating back onto the beach. They would then be caught by two Balinese guys who would guide the chute to a slow, graceful stop. The opposite happened.

The boat brought me close to the beach, but my grip partially closed the chute, which increased the speed and angle of my descent. The guys on the beach noticed this and yelled in alarm, causing several of their colleagues to rush to the landing zone to help catch me. I don't know what was said exactly as I don't speak Balinese but I think it was the equivalent of 'He's coming in hot!' Or, at least I hope it was.

Another thing to note is that Balinese men are quite slight and I'm, well, not.

The net result was I came roaring in at Mach-ten with all the grace of a charging hippopotamus and hit the landing crew like a wrecking ball. Eula's eloquent description was that poor little Balinese guys went flying through the air like skittles.

I smashed into the beach at speed, and the scene quickly resembled a disaster movie. The chute chords had wrapped around my body, causing the material to flap wildly in the breeze, and the sand was littered with an array of moaning bodies. But those brave wee guys had slowed me and the crash, while spectacular, wasn't as damaging as it could have been (for me anyway). I ended up with some mild grazing, a wrenched shoulder, and a mouthful of sand.

Once untangled, the ultra-polite Balinese crew apologised profusely for what had happened. They shouldn't have. It was my fault. I could have let go of the straps at any time, but it never occurred to me. It was my first time flying, and I was holding on as tightly as I could. As we walked quickly away, purposefully not looking at the limping crew behind us, Eula hissed out of the side of her mouth, "And that's why you're not allowed to do a parachute jump."

The rest of our Balinese trip passed without further notable incidents. Ubud was nice but a bit 'Yoga Retreat' for me.

Side note—a very bendy friend recently tried to teach me yoga, claiming it would be good for me. It wasn't. Which reinforced what I already knew. I have the flexibility of cement.

While in Ubud, I took a walk through some very picturesque rice paddies. My stroll was spoiled somewhat when I remembered that snakes often reside in rice fields. There are several venomous snakes in the area, including the deadly pit viper and spitting cobra. I got out of there quickly, but to be honest, I was half hoping to see one as I think snakes are cool and it would have made a much better story.

And that was Ubud. Calm, relaxing, a bit hippy, slightly boring and a peaceful conclusion to my first Balinese experience.

Well, that's anti-climactic. I knew I should have ended on the parachute debacle.

CHAPTER SEVEN

THE EL NINJA SEWING AND BABYWEAR SHOP

Miami and Belize 1997. Fortunately for me, Simon, my travelling companion in Central America, kept a very entertaining and detailed diary of the trip. I also have an album of embarrassing photos chronicling our adventures, so was able to blackmail him into lending it to me.

Let's skip ahead to 1997. I was working in an advertising agency as a copywriter. A job I loved (and still do, though it has become gradually less fun in line with the world being overrun by the joy police). I was 36 and Eula and I had been married for nearly ten years.

Advertising copywriters usually work with art directors and my partner at the time was an Englishman named Simon. He was quintessentially English, a similar age to me, and had a great sense of humour. The two of us got on very well, which was lucky because the ad agency we worked for was run by an A-Grade asshat.

To escape said asshat, Simon and I disappeared to the other side of the world and explore the jungles and Mayan ruins found in Belize and Guatemala.

Why there? Good question. If only I had an answer.

As with the majority of my travel decisions, I think we went to those locations because they sounded cool. As strategies go, it's not a bad one, but both our wives didn't agree with our logic and expressed zero interest in the location so, Boy's Trip!

Tell me a bit about Belize, I hear you ask. Righto then. Belize is a Caribbean country on the northeast coast of Central America. It's bordered by Mexico to the north, the Caribbean Sea to the east and Guatemala to the south and west (thanks Wikipedia). It's the least populated and least densely populated country in Central America and is the only Central American country where English is the official language. This would definitely come in handy, as that is what I speak.

As far as history goes, it has some. The Mayans popped in for a look around 1500 BC and hung around until 900 AD, then a succession of Europeans arrived to ruin it all. Cue biffo and disease. Then lots of other stuff happened up until today. There you go. All caught up.

Reading the last few sentences, I wonder if I should become a historian. Given my in-depth research, pinpoint factual accuracy and technical writing skills, I'd be a shoo-in.

Mainly, Simon and I wanted to see Mayan stuff, check out some monkeys and go diving. Boy, did we go to the right place.

Before we go further, let me reiterate that I'm relying on photos, Simon, and my hazy memories of the trip. My travel journal was lost again, so I'll be mainly winging it. But who cares, right? It'll be fun. And given the name of the book, this shouldn't be a huge surprise.

To get to Belize, you have to go through Miami. Well, you probably don't have to, but we did. My overriding memories of South Beach are sun, sand, skimpy clothes (on people who look good in skimpy clothes, not Simon or I), rollerbladers and a buzzy atmosphere.

Whilst there, we also checked out the art déco masterpiece that was the Delano South Beach Hotel. This unexpectedly cosmopolitan move was entirely down to Simon. As I said, he was an art director and was very interested in design and architecture. I, on the other hand, didn't give a rip.

To entice me along, he told me that Madonna owned the hotel and that we might see her there. While factually incorrect—she co-owned the Blue Door restaurant inside the Delano—it did the trick. I'm always up for a bit of star spotting. Not that we saw any, but the hotel itself was very cool.

When it was first constructed, the four-wing art déco tower was the tallest in Miami Beach and the hotel was originally used for military housing. It was renovated in 1994 with the décor created by someone Simon admired, renowned French designer Phillipe Starck.

The hotel was the sort of place where the beautiful people (and us) hung out. I remember it mostly as the bar where I first heard the song Glory Box by Portishead. A great song by itself, but it fitted the ambience perfectly.

Well played DJ Whoeverthehellyouwere. Smashed it.

Next stop, Belize City. Almost exactly the same as Miami Beach, except for everything. There were no rollerblading people in the streets, mainly because the roads were made of dirt and catastrophe would have followed. We'd gone from first-world excesses to developing country basics in one short plane ride.

Upon doing a bit of reading (Glenn 'Research' Wood) I found out that Belize City is not only the largest in the country but it's also been spectacularly unlucky with natural disasters. It's been directly struck by two hurricanes since 1900 and hit hard by two others. At various times, areas of the city have also been burnt down. In an ironic twist, it's also susceptible to flooding. Booking the movers now.

What the city had, however, was the EL NINJA sewing and babywear shop. I don't know why no one has thought to combine deadly martial arts with infant's wear before, but in my opinion, it's a sure-fire winner.

The logo featured black-clad, kicking, ninja warriors and throwing stars plus, incongruously, a sewing bobbin. That's just excellent.

According to the sign, they sold sewing accessories, cosmetics, babywear and interior clothing. Just what happens to interior clothing if you take it outside, it didn't say. Nothing good, I suspect. Sadly, it was closed, so further inspection was impossible, but I really hope it becomes a chain.

We weren't in the city just to peruse children's wear. We were there to meet up with the group we'd be travelling with.

As we were journeying to remote areas, Simon and I decided we'd be better off with a hardened group of fellow explorers. That way, we could have each other's backs during the expeditions. We'd booked with an adventure tour company that looked suitably hard core and were excited to meet our travel group.

I speculated that, as we were close to the USA, we'd probably have some marines in our squad and maybe a scattering of extreme-sport athletes plus mercenaries on the run from Johnny Law.

Ranulph Fiennes would probably be there as well.

The meeting was scheduled for midday in a local hotel. Simon and I arrived on the dot of twelve, but something was amiss. We seemed to have stumbled into an old folk's home by accident. Almost everyone in the room was over seventy. We went back outside and checked the address. According to our itinerary, we were in the right place. Confused, we hurried back inside. The octogenarians were still there, drinking tea and talking about hip operations. We reasoned there must have been a second conference room; the one we were in was obviously hosting an incontinence symposium, so there must have been another where all the marines and adventurers were hanging out.

Yeah, nah. We were in the right place.

For reasons that are still unclear, most bookings for our tour were from pensioners. Call it bad luck, call it God having a laugh, but the trip we'd reserved had obviously coincided with a rest home escape. There were two or three other travellers under forty in the group and they were looking equally nonplussed, as were the Belize nationals who had been hired to lead the expedition.

Stan, the bus driver, was a big, cool-looking dude in his thirties and the tour leader. Mary was a fit, capable woman in her mid-twenties. She had a huge smile and a wicked sense of humour. At that moment, she was looking more concerned than amused. Clearly, she hadn't expected the average age of the tour group to be one-hundred-and-seven.

She called us together and once the clattering of walking frames had subsided, began outlining the itinerary. Mary emphasised that there would be a fair amount of walking and some climbing over difficult obstacles involved in the tour. Looking at the assembled crowd with trepidation, she asked if everyone thought they were up to the challenge. At that exact moment, one of the senior citizens hit the floor with a dramatic thud.

'Christ,' I thought sympathetically, 'one of the oldsters has had a heart attack and we haven't even left the hotel!'

A concerned crowd surrounded the woman who had passed out. She came too quickly, and it was apparent she had fainted rather than had a major medical event. She was given water and helped to her feet. The tropical heat and dehydration were blamed for the collapse, though I'm sure her being older than space dust played a part.

It was not a great start to the tour. We were here to see ancient ruins but didn't expect them to be in our group!

Viewing our transport didn't help. We would be travelling the country in a dilapidated bus rented from a company called Batty's. As in, you'd be batty to ride in it.

Before we could be herded into the bus, I took Mary aside for a quick word. I explained that Simon and I were looking for an adventure and were concerned that our aged fellow travellers might put a dampener on things. Mary was sympathetic. She explained that our best approach would be to treat the tour as transport only and not join the guided portions of the trip. That way, the bus would get us to the places we wanted to go and then we'd be free to explore on our own.

This was great advice. We would happily chat with the other members of the group en route, then be left to our own devices until it was time to get back on the bus. On most occasions, Mary would sit with us while travelling and give us a breakdown of what we were about to see. That way, we could capitalise on her local knowledge without having to trundle around with the group to get it, which would have driven us mad.

I have nothing against the elderly (I'm not far off it myself) but our group was very slow and weren't likely to cut their own paths through the jungle or climb the Mayan temples as we wished to.

Our first stop was Altan Ha, an archaeological site that uncovered the ruins of an ancient Mayan City about fifty kilometres north of Belize City. Like a lot of the Mayan ruins, the site was dominated by pyramid-shaped temples, stone altars, masonry carvings and burial chambers.

It was well cool.

Simon and I romped around the site, offending the gods at every turn. Simon played the part of a sacrificial virgin (unconvincingly) on one altar and we'd made it to the top of the sixteen-metre-high 'Temple of The Masonry Altars' before the rest of the group had made it out of the bus.

Fun Fact: A drawing of the aforementioned temple features on the logo of Belize's leading beer brand—Belikin. What the ancient Mayan civilisation has to do with beer, I'm not sure. I can confirm through research (Google again) that the Mayans brewed a beer-like substance and, having drunk it, agree that Belikin is also a beer-like substance, so let's go with that.

There's some conjecture as to which particular god the main temple was erected for. Initially, it was thought to be the Sun God *Kinich Ahau,* who, according to legend, will put an end to the world by descending from the heavens and having his jaguars devour mankind.

So, not a great guy then.

However, people who know more than me (almost everyone) have suggested that the temple may have been built to worship a Jester God, who sounds like a much more fun dude. I have a photo of a stone carving which is definitely poking out its tongue, so, you know, case closed.

While poor old Mary herded the pensioners towards the temples, Simon and I disappeared into the jungle behind the official site. We found that exploring the area around the tourist sites was often more fascinating than the sanctioned zones. This way, we came across ruins that were yet to be properly excavated and were overgrown by the jungle. It was like we were discovering them for the first time.

In this particular site, we also discovered a tarantula lurking under a rock we had overturned. I'm pretty sure it was a Mayan tarantula and, therefore, had heritage status. We decided not to mess with it because, well, aside from being a national treasure, it was large, terrifying and looked quite pissed off.

Having narrowly escaped the deadly arachnid, we re-joined the tour and travelled to the Crooked Tree Bird and Wildlife Sanctuary. At least, I think we did. I'm basing this off the order. I placed my photographs in an album so it's not a fool-proof system. However, it's all we have.

We got to Crooked Tree by boat, which is always fun, especially when the boats are run by local fishermen. I have a photo of a young boy displaying his catch to me and, I can't be certain, but they look suspiciously like piranhas. So much for a late afternoon dip in the river.

The sanctuary itself was beautiful, not in a Caribbean Island, swaying palm trees sort of way, but in a vibrant jungle ecosystem style. The sanctuary contains over sixteen thousand acres of lagoons, creeks, swamps, forests and pine savanna and is home to hundreds of species of wildlife. It's also a waterfowl habitat and nesting site for the rare Jabiru stork. I'm pretty sure we didn't see any, as they are large and have distinctive red markings on their lower neck.

You'd think I'd remember that, but I'm not really a bird guy and if you've seen one stork, you've seen 'em all.

Our accommodation in the reserve was certainly authentic. By this I mean a raised hut with thin, wooden log walls and a thatched roof. I remember walking in behind Simon and studying his reaction. Remember, this is a man used to designer furniture and five-star accommodation. He took one look at the bare walls and bunk beds, turned to me and said, "There's nowhere to hang your anorak."

Once an Englishman, always an Englishman.

CHAPTER EIGHT

PREHENSILE AND PREHISTORIC PENISES

Belize 1997. Memories courtesy of my brain and Simon's diary. For an art director, he really is a very good writer.

So, we've established that my English friend Simon and I are in Belize and that Simon has an anorak. Dilemma of dilemmas, he also has nowhere to hang it.

I know that's a shocking revelation, but that's just the kind of book this is.

Bravely putting aside the lack of clothes hooks, Simon rallied, and we prepared ourselves for a trip down the Belize River en route to the Mesoamerican archaeological site of Lamanai. The name means submerged crocodile in Yucatec Maya, so no frolicking in the waters by the temple.

Lamanai is one of the oldest, continuously inhabited archaeological zones in the Mayan world. It is also one of only a handful of sites to keep its original name. The park covers 384 hectares and is the second largest in Belize. Most of the site is unrestored, which meant there was much to explore for those with two working hips.

Upon arrival, Simon and I ditched the oldies once again and

employed our 'disappear into the jungle, ignore all the cleared trails and approach the ruins like marauding conquistadors' approach. It worked a treat. We emerged at the rear of the high temple and, to our delight, discovered a bat cave, not *the* bat cave obviously, though this would have been a brilliant place for Bruce Wayne to hide.

We've lit the bat signal where the hell is Batman? Give him a minute, he's hit traffic in Mexico.

Okay, perhaps not. Anyway, our bat cave contained something even better than the bat-mobile—an old, dead guy.

At first, I thought the Belize sun had finally overcome one of our tour group, but fortunately, they were all still milling around by the bus. No, this dead guy was actually the mummified remains of one of the Mayan elite. His tomb was still in the process of being exhumed and, amazingly, hadn't been roped off or had access restricted in any way. It was, however, protected by a significant population of large, active bats.

I'm not a fan.

Flappy, screeching, disease-carrying, flying ratopaths. My term (which I'm quite proud of) for a psychopathic flying rat and I think I'm justified in using it here. I don't trust any of them. Even their poo is dangerous—more on this later.

Simon and I had a quick poke around in the corpse cave, but there was quite a lot of frenzied bat action, so we got out before we got bitten, scratched, or became too freaked out.

Leaving the Mayan mummy in peace, we climbed to the top of one of the temples. We had a brilliant view of the surrounding jungle, looking all the way to the river and while bush bashing to the next ruin (there were three major structures—The Temple of the Masks, The High Temple and the Jaguar Temple) we were stoked to find the trees inhabited with black howler monkeys.

I love those dudes.

They didn't seem at all bothered by us and were chillaxing in the trees as we walked past. I remember seeing a mum and her baby hanging by her toes, upside down on a vine, just a few metres from me. Their cry added a really spooky vibe to the area.

Howler monkeys are widely considered to be the world's loudest land animals. According to the Guinness Book of World Records, their calls can be heard clearly for four point eight kilometres. Their main vocals consist of loud, deep guttural growls, but despite sounding frankly terrifying, they're generally not aggressive. We certainly never felt threatened by them.

The next temple we 'discovered' was the jaguar temple, which had an intricate rock jaguar mask sculpted into the rock at the bottom left of the structure.

One of the disadvantages of not sticking with the tour group was we didn't get any background knowledge about the places we were viewing. Neither Simon nor I had bothered doing any research pre-trip so, unless we asked afterwards, we didn't really learn much.

At this particular temple, my lack of knowledge was probably a good thing. I found out later that, according to legend, hidden somewhere in the ruins, is an ancient spear called *the heart of the jaguar*. If I'd known this, I'd have spent all of my time looking for it.

I would also have worked out its magical properties. Nothing so boring as turning the wielder into a jaguar-type beast. Hell no. In my version of the story, when I hold the heart of the jaguar spear, my actual heart is replaced by a jaguar's heart which gives me super prowling skills and, most importantly, the Brain Bite of Death ability. Jaguars can bite directly through the skull of their prey between their ears and deliver a fatal blow to the brain. Now that's a superpower!

Sadly, I knew nothing about the spear, so it remains undiscovered to this day. I also struggle to bite through particularly crusty bread, so am pretty sure the powers didn't transfer to me and remain secreted in the jaguar temple. Bugger.

Our next stop was the Belize Zoo, which bills itself as the best little zoo in the world. This is a big call, but I have fond memories of it for various reasons, which we'll get to shortly.

I generally don't like zoos. I know why they are important and realise modern zoos are different from the ones I remember as a kid. Back then, big animals would pace around in small cages. I found them to be depressing places and have always preferred to see animals in the wild. I could go off on a massive conservation-themed rant here but you can easily work out what I'm going to say and, really, an in-depth discussion on environmentalism is better left to the experts.

The Belize Zoo opened in 1983 as a last-ditch effort to provide a home for a collection of wild animals which had been used in making documentary films about tropical forests—irony much? It's a non-governmental, non-profit organisation focusing on wildlife conservation through rehabilitation and environmental education. It is made up of animals that were orphaned, rescued, born at the zoo, rehabilitated, or sent from other zoological institutions.

Its vibe is best captured by the wording on this sign I photographed while there. I'm quoting it verbatim, including punctuation and the fact that it's all in caps.

I AM AN ORNATE HAWK-EAGLE, AND SOMEONE SHOT ME! YES MON! SHOT ME! AND LOOK YA! NOT MANY COUNTRIES HAVE BIRDS AS BIG AND AS PRETTY AS WE ORNATE HAWK-EAGLES. LISTEN MY SPECIES LOVES TO EAT SNAKES! NOT LIKE YOU! AND MY SPECIES LOVES BELIZE!! JUST LIKE YOU!

Nine exclamation marks. Nine! (ten including that one). What did the ornate Hawk-eagle look like, I hear you ask? I dunno, I couldn't find it. Mind you, it has a pretty good excuse to hide from humans.

Having seen the sign, I assumed (incorrectly) that the zoo had a pretty chilled attitude to visitor interaction with the critters.

Now, I know better than to feed the animals but if you come across a coatimundi (my absolute favourite diurnal mammal) that's looking a bit thirsty then surely sticking your water bottle through the fence to give it a drink is okay, right? Apparently not. I got a serious dressing down from one of the keepers who immediately placed me in the irresponsible tourist category—yeah, fair call. I wasn't threatened with expulsion, but they kept a close eye on me after that.

The main reason I remember Belize Zoo so vividly is the Tapir.

Or more specifically, the tapir's penis. Before we get onto the penis, so to speak, let's talk a bit about the tapir itself.

Tapir are large herbivorous mammals, similar in shape to a pig but with a short nose trunk, which can be used as a snorkel. Interesting so far, but not OMG memorable. Although they often live in dryland forests, tapirs like to frolic in waterways if they are close by (don't we all). When entering a river, tapirs will swim, sink to the bottom and walk along the riverbed to feed.

Much as I'd like to see that it's still way less interesting than their dongs. About that.

The tapir has a gigantic prehensile penis.

Terrifyingly, prehensile means it can grip with it. It is literally a gripping penis. I mean, how useful would that be? Hands full with bags of groceries and you need to open the car door? Do it with your penis. Of course, there's a high likelihood of instant arrest, but aside from that, it'd be brilliant.

As tapirs don't drive cars, they use their mammoth, grabbing penises to hold on to female tapirs during copulation, thus ensuring insemination but probably signalling the end of the romance. You used to send me flowers, now you just pin me down with your penis! Ahh, the wonders of nature.

Simon and I had the good fortune (or misfortune, depending on your point of view) to observe a tapir penis up close. At first, I thought a huge python had snuck into the tapir's cage and was eating its leg, but no, it was his willy. It's so long that there is video footage of tapirs using their appendage to scratch their backs. Best party trick ever and quite a thing to see.

I wouldn't advise googling it, though, as I think I've now been placed on several Interpol watch lists.

It's interesting to note that female tapirs are pregnant for thirteen or fourteen months. I assume that's because they are in no hurry to have sex again. Can't say I blame them.

Upon leaving the zoo, our intrepid tour leaders took us west, heading towards the unpronounceable ruins of Xunantunich.

Things get a little foggy here. My next photograph is of Simon sitting in the tray of a ute as we drive along. I have no memory of this. Why are we in a ute? What happened to the tour bus? Where are Stan, Mary and the octogenarians? Even more oddly, the photo after this is of a large bull lying in a dusty field. Directly behind him is a tree full of vultures so, you'd have to say things are not looking good. In the Disney version, the bull is sleeping. In the real world, he's dead and is about to become vulture chow.

In trying to put all of this together I've decided Stan hit the bull with the bus, putting it out of commission (the bus and the bull) and we were loaded onto a selection of emergency vehicles rounded up by locals to evacuate us to our next location. A bit like Dunkirk, but with fewer Stukas. Or a more likely answer is Mary loaded Simon and me on to a mate's vehicle and sent us into town to get supplies, as we were the only ones able-bodied enough to make the trip. That's ringing a bell.

One thing I remember about the journey west was how dry the countryside was. There were also wisps of smoke in the distance. I asked Mary about it and she said there had been a lot of fires in Belize recently. The biggest one had been started by the sun refracting off a discarded bottle of Coca-Cola and setting the scrub alight. Coke don't put that in the adverts.

On to Xunantunich aka the Maiden of the Rock, so named for the ghost of a woman, claimed to haunt the site. She is dressed completely in white and has fire-red glowing eyes. What is it with ghosts and fashion? They always seem to appear in white, black, or occasionally red. For once, I'd like to see one turn up in jeans and a light blue t-shirt, possibly with a smiley face on the front. I think that would set the fire-red eyes off nicely.

Apparently, Ghosty girl turns up in front of 'El Castillo'—the main temple at Xunantunich—ascends the stone stairs and disappears into the wall. She's been doing this since 1892, so she must be getting sick of it by now. On the day we were there, she must have been taking a break because she didn't show up. Disappointing.

Xunantunich was the biggest set of ruins we visited in Belize. The core of the city covers two point six kilometres and consists of a series of six plazas containing over twenty-six temples and palaces. 'El Castillo' is the second tallest structure in Belize at over forty metres in height. It's an important site as Xunantunich was expanding its power and reach, while most other Mayan civilisations were crumbling. It lasted nearly a century longer than most other sites in the region, but the thing I remember most about it is fiberglass.

When we visited, the main temple (El Castillo) was looking pretty shabby. There were warning signs on the front of it and you weren't allowed to climb it, unlike the other ruins we'd visited. The one thing that was still in good nick was a band of impressive Mayan carvings or friezes that were prominent on the base of the structure. The carvings depicted the birth and lives of several gods, as well as a segment dedicated to the tree of life.

On closer inspection, some sections were in much better condition than others—some were heavily worn and stained black by the weather and decay, while others were clean and sharp. I assumed that the unstained areas had been restored, but Mary told us that a lot of the friezes had actually been reconstructed with plaster and fiberglass moulds.

Simon and I were pretty disenchanted. I understand why they were doing it, but I prefer my ruins. Well, umm, ruined.

Speaking of ruined. The biggest shock of the day came at lunchtime, when the whole group was taken to a nearby pool for a refreshing dip. Simon and I used strategically placed towels to change into our swimming trunks. Several of the older members of our party had no such concern for modesty. They stripped off right in front of us, flashing antiquated genitalia around with gay abandon. Some parts reminded me of a wizened version of the tapir's nose trunk, others a pile of overcooked French crepes. Even though my brain was screaming for me to look away, I remained transfixed and the images burned into my brain. Judging by Simon's dropped jaw and expression of horror, he was experiencing similar emotions.

Some things you can't un-see.

CHAPTER NINE

A QUICK DETOUR TO YAVIN 4

Belize and Guatemala 1997. Is it accurate to say that this diary was actually lost, as clearly Simon still has it? He lives on the other side of the world to me, so I'm going with it. There's no point arguing.

I like a good cave. I mean, who doesn't?

This was fortunate, as The Rio Frio caves were our next stop in Belize. They were excellent. The caves were grotto-like and contained everything you'd want from a large hole in the ground. The entrance was massive, over twenty metres high, and just inside the opening were huge multicoloured boulders and gigantic stalactites, hanging from the ceiling like enormous vampire teeth.

It was pitch black inside and incredibly eerie. There were, of course, the ever-present bats nestled high in the ceiling. I ventured by myself down a particularly dark passageway and just as I was getting nervous about how far I'd strayed from the group, a ghostly shape appeared on a rock shelf above me and launched into the air, wailing like a banshee. This scared the absolute crap out of me. My head was screaming for me to run, but my feet stayed firmly rooted to the spot. This did not bode well for any future wild animal attack.

The apparition landed in a puff of dust right next to me and burst into a fit of laughter. It was Mary, the tour guide. She'd been hiding on the ledge for ten minutes, waiting for an unsuspecting member of the group to come along. I suspect this wasn't the first time she'd done this. Once my heartbeat had returned to just elevated, I congratulated her on an excellent joke—I'm nothing if not a good sport—then suggested it may not be a great idea to play the same trick on the more senior members of the group. It would be quite difficult to get a corpse out of the cavern. Mary gave a wide smile and assured me she'd been waiting for Simon or me, the only ones she thought were likely to venture this deep into the caves. Lucky me.

Mary was quite a character and had gone out of her way to make sure everyone on the tour had a good time. She hadn't spent much time with me or Simon as we were happy to be left to our own devices, but her good humour and youthful enthusiasm kept the mood light, even during hard travelling days.

She was also a mine of information. Mary obviously loved her country and had carefully researched the places we went. It is only now that I'm retracing our tour that I realise how well thought out our itinerary was. They really did take us to all the best attractions and also gave us a genuine taste of the country as well as some excellent off-the-beaten-track experiences.

Not all the facts Mary imparted were positive. As we walked back through the cavern, we came across an area that was stained with bat guano. I shone the torch on it to get a better look. Mary warned me not to get too close. She told me that bat crap is lethal stuff. It contains all sorts of viruses, including some airborne ones and some caves which contained high deposits of bat poo were quite dangerous.

There is some speculation that COVID came from bat guano. This wasn't an issue in 1997, but it sure as hell is today.

Recently, six completely new coronaviruses were discovered in samples of bat manure, which is excellent news. Scientists have been trying to work out how these viruses might spread to humans.

It is thought transmission could occur from a bite, but bats don't generally chew on humans, so some good news there. That doesn't last. Instead, humans mostly get infected by bats simply by spending time with them. This contact usually comes in the form of workers collecting guano from caves (it's a sought-after ingredient in fertilisers and some Chinese medicines), or when spelunkers or miners spend hours breathing in the same confined space as a bat colony. So, exactly like we were doing in Belize.

To my knowledge, neither Simon nor I became infected, or maybe we did. It would certainly explain a few things.

Having made it out of the caves alive and probably uninfected, it was time to leave Belize and pop over to Guatemala to visit the legendary archaeological site of Tikal.

That's not complicated at all, is it?

Actually, yes, it is because according to Guatemala we'd never been in Belize at all but had actually been in their sovereign territory the whole time. Confused? Simon and I certainly were.

Let me explain. Belize and Guatemala are in a territory dispute and have been since oh, I dunno, the late 1600s. Some countries really know how to hold a grudge.

Here's how that came about. Britain and Spain are involved (of course they are). In the 1700s, both countries signed several treaties regarding territories in the Americas. Both nations agreed that the territory of modern-day Belize was under Spanish sovereignty, but English settlers could use the land, with a few caveats; only for donkey farming and cheese rolling (I may have made that up, but who can tell?). Anyway, the area was never fully under Spanish or British control.

When the Spanish Empire fell (1820-ish) the Guatemalans, knowing an opportunity when they saw one, said they inherited Spanish rights over the territory. Kind of like an ancient form of calling 'shotgun.' Since then, Guatemala has in whole, or in part, claimed the territory of Belize.

This has caused a lot of Argy Bargy over the years as the Poms weren't having a bar of it. Words were had, notes were exchanged, names were called (the term poo-face may have been used, that's never been confirmed). There was some drunk texting, treaties were voided, negotiations failed, invasion threats were issued, troops were stationed at the border, yadda yadda.

Things calmed down a bit when Belize gained its independence in 1981 and then flared up again in 1999 when Guatemala brought up the whole inheritance of Spanish claims thing again and wanted to take over the southern half of Belize. As late as November 2022, the dispute is still going through the courts with no resolution in sight.

We were there in 1997, and Guatemala was firing up for the claims to come in 1999. We knew this because, on crossing the border, we were met by a horrifying billboard depicting the head of a fierce half-monkey, half-man wearing a black mask. He wore a red beret and the word **ATREVETE!** was written underneath, which translates to "I dare you" in Spanish.

So, that's not great.

We were told that guerrillas had been active in the border region, but I heard *gorillas* and was initially quite excited. In reality, raiding parties had been seen in the area and threats had been made to tour groups crossing over from Belize—as we were.

Mary was typically philosophical about it all. No attacks had been made.... yet. By her reasoning, no problem. Simon and I figured that, in the event of an emergency, we could easily outrun most of the group, so we should be sweet. I saw a map on the Guatemalan side of the border, which didn't show Belize at all. The whole country was incorporated into Guatemala. These dudes were serious.

However, we were not there to get involved in political shenanigans. We were there to see the rebel base Yavin 4 from *Star Wars: Episode IV. A New Hope*.

Does that make us appear like geeks? Nah, we just sound cool.

Okay, more clarification if I must. The ancient Mayan pyramids in the Tikal National Park in Guatemala were used to film several shots from the *Star Wars* movie. In the film, we see a Rebel supervising the landing of the Millennium Falcon. The shot was taken on top of a building imaginatively known as Temple Four. It looks east towards the equally creatively named Temples One, Two and Three. I'm pretty sure the Mayans had much better names. Tikal itself may have been called Yax Mutal, which is much better and actually sounds like a character from *Star Wars.*

"Who stole the plans for the twenty-seventh Death Star?"

"We're not sure, but the prime suspect is Yax Mutal from Oglene Twelve."

I could totally have written *Star Wars*. If anyone knows Mr Lucas, please pass on my name.

Back to Tikal. It's one of the largest archaeological sites and urban centres of pre-Columbian Mayan civilisation and a UNESCO World Heritage Site. It goes way back—three hundred BC ish. I could give you the exact dates and details, but you're not here for a history lesson. You're here for a good time.

Are you not entertained?

We were. The ruins were incredible. They sit amongst the vibrant, tropical rainforest teeming with life. Some of the cool critters we could have seen included white-nosed coatis, grey foxes, spider monkeys, howler monkeys, harpy eagles, falcons, ocellated turkeys, guans, toucans, parrots and leafcutter ants. Jaguar, Ocelots and cougar also stalk the park. Naturally, we didn't see all of these creatures, but we ticked quite a few off the list.

Not that we were there for the wildlife. It was just the cherry on the top of an incredible day. The ruins were sprawling, awe-inspiring, eerie, well-preserved and open for exploration. We could pretty much wander wherever we wanted, including temples in the jungle that were still overgrown and unexcavated. Not that you needed to explore outside the main site. There was so much to see. In fact, there are thousands of ancient structures on the site and only a fraction of them have been uncovered.

One of the disadvantages of giving tourists such freedom is that there will always be a few cock-wombles who will fuck it up for everyone. I was absolutely disgusted to see graffiti inside some of the temples. Hey, Dave from Alabama, no one is interested in your scrawl. The fricking conquistadors were here, and they didn't feel the need to advertise the fact, okay!

A temple was closed because a tourist fell to their death from it. It seemed random to single out that particular structure for closure, as there were plenty of other places you could easily fall to your doom. I have photos of Simon negotiating a particularly hairy ledge about twenty metres off the ground. Fortunately, he is as sure-footed as a mountain goat and got down safely.

We spent a fascinating morning scrambling all over the site, filling our boots with temples, royal palaces, pyramids, residences, platforms, plazas and inscribed stone monuments. There were even seven courts uncovered that were used to play Mesoamerican ball games, which was a sport similar to racquetball, but with one core difference. It was pretty easy to die playing it.

It was played with a heavy, solid ball which did some serious damage. According to reports from the Spanish 500 years ago, bruising from the games was so severe that they had to be lanced open. Players could even be killed if the ball hit them in the mouth, stomach or intestines. In other fun news, while some games were played for simple recreation, others were formal spectacles leading to human sacrifice. Always a great end to a sporting engagement.

Simon and I were up for a game, but we couldn't find anyone else who was interested. Apparently, they all liked their intestines where they were.

It was high inside one of the temples that I saw a glorious sight outside one of the limestone windows. My first toucan.

They really are the most spectacular birds. Brightly coloured with huge beaks that can measure more than half the length of their bodies and a noisy frog-like croak that can be heard over a kilometre away. It was a real thrill to see one in the wild.

My next wildlife encounter came as I was sitting at the base of one of the temples, about to eat my lunch. A white-nosed Coati wandered out of the jungle, then sauntered over to me like we were a couple of old mates catching up for coffee. He was a very cute looking fella (I say he, but I don't know and it seemed rude to ask. We'd only just met.) and was about a metre and a half long including his tail, light brown in colour with flecks of white on his coat and a fox-like face. He had absolutely no fear of me, getting as close as half a metre away. Naturally, he was checking to see if I had any food. This wasn't his first tourist rodeo. I had my daypack sitting next to me on the ground and this super-confident animal stuck his snout right inside one of the pouches. He wasn't aggressive, but I was aware he was a wild animal, so didn't make any sudden movements, or try to pat him, even though he was very close to me. I also remembered my experience at Belize Zoo and made sure I didn't feed him, either.

Another incredible experience at Tikal.

Later that day, as Simon and I wandered through the surrounding jungle, a much larger creature dropped from the trees close to us, landing on the ground with a thud that frightened the crap out of us and then scampering away. Neither Simon nor I were sure what it was, but an educated guess would be an ape of some kind, probably a big adult Spider Monkey.

Very cool and a great way to end an extremely memorable day in Guatemala, but now it was time to get back to Belize. The tour group was obviously working on the principle that the less time spent in hostile territories, the better. A policy I fully endorse.

We didn't experience much of Guatemala's culture or see much of the country, but I will say their ancient ruins are excellent and no one shot at us.

I'm taking that as a win.

CHAPTER TEN

WHERE THE HELL ARE THE JAGUARS?

Belize 1997. Thanks to the embarrassing photos blackmailing scam (I won't describe them. I promised Simon) and subsequent access to the diaries, there's not much for me to do here. So, on with the story.

Another day, another cave.

Okay, so it was only our second cave of the trip, but it featured in the last chapter, so I'm sticking with that intro.

The cave we were taken to was called Saint Herman's Cave, which is located in Saint Herman's Blue Hole National Park. Why Saint Herman had a blue hole, I don't know. Maybe he was cold.

Come on, that gag was laid out on a silver platter. You must have seen it coming.

I wanted to know more about Saint Herman but, after extensive googling, I only found one and he lived in Alaska. Things became clearer the more I read. It seems the park was originally called the Blue Hole (snigger) National Park, but was often confused with the much more famous Great Blue Hole (snort) which is a giant marine sinkhole off the coast of Belize. So, they changed the name to Saint Herman's Blue Hole National Park. Who 'they' were and why they invented a saint is beyond me. And surely, if you are going to make up a semi-deity, you'd give them a backstory. It appears not. That's just sloppy.

Anyhoo, the caves had similar features to Rio Frio in that they were both, umm, caves.

Saint Herman's differed, however, as it had a stream running through it. The guidebooks said it was a small stream, but I beg to differ as I have a photo of Simon literally up to his chin in water.

The caves were huge and dominated by incredible limestone formations and, of course, bats. So, we had another chance to be infected with the airborne bat guano virus and this time, by golly, we were going to take it. Kidding. We came out with exactly the same amount of viruses we went in with.

It was pitch black inside the caves. Who'd have picked that? Fortunately, Simon and I were prepared—I'm pretty sure he'd been a boy scout—and we had small but powerful torches. This gave us the ultimately misplaced confidence to explore more deeply into the furthest reaches of the caverns.

"We'll be fine," said Simon, right before he got us lost.

Just before panic set in, Mary found us. We were becoming higher maintenance than the oldies. After we'd explored the cave, we elected to see the Inland Blue Hole. Well, you would, wouldn't you?

How interesting can a hole be I hear you ask? Pretty bloody interesting if it's filled with water and the current temperature is forty degrees Celsius.

The Inland Blue Hole, as opposed to the one at sea (I realise how confusing this might be now), is a sapphire-coloured sinkhole that forms an eight-metre-deep swimming lake fed by an underground cave system that flows into the Sibun River.

It's a forty-five-minute hike through dense jungle to get there. Or you could drive to the car park and walk five minutes down a gentle track.

Guess which option the oldies took. Now, guess which Simon and I went for.

There are no prizes for the correct answer.

Several things happened on the trek. First, Simon announced he was going to relieve himself against a nearby tree. Several seconds into the act, he turned back towards me and yelled, "Come and have a look at this giant lizard."

I immediately burst out laughing and said I wanted nothing to do with his lizard.

He started laughing as well, which threw off his aim and the innocent reptile walking nearby may have been affected. Whether or not it was showered in urine, Simon couldn't confirm, but it took off suspiciously quickly and thus remained unseen by me. If it ever existed in the first place.

The other thing that happened was we both saw our first hummingbirds.

Hummingbirds are well cool. They are tiny, between eight and thirteen centimetres in length, and move incredibly quickly—like a bee on speed. They hover in mid-air by flapping their wings at a tremendous pace, up to eighty times per second, and can fly at over 50 kilometres per hour.

The thing that struck us was the sound they made. Their wings flap at high frequencies that are audible to humans and they create a definite humming sound; thus, the name hummingbird. That really was a no-brainer.

On an almost literal buzz from our hummingbird sightings, we were worried that the pools would let us down. They didn't; they were awesome. The water was blue, as advertised, and the temperature was refreshing, especially after our humid slog through the jungle and, best of all, there were high cliffs to jump off.

When it comes to swimming holes, having some sort of promontory to leap off is a must. I am reasonably careful to check the depth of the landing zone and also ensure it is free of submerged debris. Surprisingly sensible, I know!

I'm comfortable jumping off heights of between 6 to 10 metres, but get wobbly above that. The world record is 58.8 metres and the lunatic who did it (Laso Schaller) hit a speed of 123 kilometres per hour before entering the water. That's truly impressive and completely nutso. It must have been like jumping into concrete.

The next stop in our Belizean Odyssey was the Cockscomb Basin Wildlife Sanctuary and jaguar preserve (not the car). This unique sanctuary covers over one-hundred-and-fifty square miles of tropical forest and is the world's only jaguar preserve.

I was very excited about this, as finding a jaguar was high on my 'things to see' checklist. Actually, any cat bigger than a moggy would have done.

Here's how well I've done with big cat spotting in the wild so far.

Lion—Nope. Tiger- Nope. Puma—Nope. Leopard—not on your nelly. Cheetah—Yeah. Nah. Panther—thought I might have caught a glimpse of one in Bodmin but unconfirmed. I've also failed to see bobcats, lynx, serval and ocelots.

Sure, I've seen them in zoos, but that's not the same.

Simon was equally excited and the two of us set off into the jungle, machetes at the ready to ward off the swarms of jaguars that were bound to be coming our way.

We hadn't accounted for the fact that jaguars are masters of stealth, unlike the two of us. In fact, their very existence relies on them being able to see their prey (us) but not being seen themselves. I can tell you right now, they are very good at it because Simon and I didn't catch so much as a glimpse. We tramped around the so-called jaguar trail for several hours, desperately looking but failing to see anything other than the rather unimpressive jungle.

When we returned to the entrance, we spoke to one of the guides and expressed our disappointment at the complete lack of jaguars on the jaguar trail. He didn't appear surprised. He told us that sightings were very rare and only happened at night. Why then, for god's sake, were we encouraged to stumble around in the blinding light of the day looking for an animal that only came out at night? We asked if it was possible to do a night tour and were told they didn't do them. Of course they didn't. That would have been far too sensible and may have resulted in people who paid to see a jaguar actually seeing one.

We also found out that the odds of us seeing a jaguar were seventeen thousand to one. If we'd known this, we'd probably have managed our expectations and purchased tickets for the Tyrannosaurus Rex tour instead.

If you're going to be crushingly disappointed, you might as well do it big.

Maybe, just maybe, someone might have mentioned all of this before we headed off, or perhaps they could have renamed the park the Cockscomb Basin Wildlife Sanctuary and Impossible to Spot Jaguar Preserve. Not catchy, I'll agree, but accurate.

The things we did find in the park were ants. Lots of ants. Big, swarmy, bitey, ants.

I didn't realise just how much ants could suck until I discovered the ants of other countries.

In New Zealand, ants are alright. I wouldn't go out of my way to be friends with them, but I don't actively dislike them. Sure, they are annoying at barbecues (they burn the sausages) and when you get a column of them in the house, it's aggravating but Kiwi ants aren't actively trying to terminate your existence.

The same can't be said for some of their international cousins.

Naturally, several of the world's most deadly ants can be found in Australia. Of course they can. Where else would they live?

The Jack jumper ant, aka, the Jack jumper, jumping jack, hopper ant or jumper ant, is extremely poisonous and native to Aussie. It's big, mean, aggressive, and potentially deadly, so it fits in well with the rest of Australia's wildlife. It is one of the few ant species that can be dangerous to humans, with its venom able to bring about an anaphylactic reaction in some people. Between 1980 and 2000, four deaths have been recorded in Tasmania due to Jack jumper stings.

Not content with having the Jack jumper, Australia also has the bulldog ant, which vies for the top spot in the suckiest ant competition.

The bulldog ant is super aggressive and can use its stinger and jaw at the same time, so double the fun. Its venom can kill a full-grown man in fifteen minutes. Super.

Death by two ant varieties. Well done, Australia.

East and Central Africa also score highly as they are home to safari ants. These guys and girls (I assume) are super swarmers. A colony on the march pretty much obliterates everything in its path, consuming up to fifty thousand prey animals a day. Frankly, that's terrifying and a solid reason not to get in their way.

I've had a personal encounter with the next bastard ant. The Fire ant. I disturbed a nest while in Borneo and can confirm what absolute pricks they were. When agitated, they swarm and release a pheromone that makes more ants want to attack. Well, hell!

They have an extremely painful sting, which creates an initial burning sensation that turns into a swollen, itchy bump. Fire ant. I'd fire the lot of them!

Very proud of that Dad Joke.

Our final entrant in the ant arsehole gallery is the bullet ant, which holds the record for the most painful sting. The bullet ant lives in South America and is also known as the twenty-four-hour ant because, wait for it, you can feel the pain of its bite for up to twenty-four hours after being stung. Other reactions to its venom include swelling, limb paralysis and uncontrollable shaking. Some victims have described that being stung by the bullet ant is as painful as being shot, hence the name. None of that sounds even remotely pleasant.

There are also crazy ants, which are ... crazy and big-headed ants which have big heads.

Ants eh! Who knew they'd produce such a wealth of comic and dramatic material?

I'm not sure what variety we ran into in the wilds of Cockscomb. Both fire ants and bullet ants live there, but they were more swarming than painful. Or maybe we got lucky because we were wearing hard-core tramping boots.

Here's how Simon describes the incident:

"We were walking along a jungle trail and I vividly recall seeing a swarm of ants crawling up your legs because you were in front of me. I looked down at my legs and there was nothing there. I said you should probably walk a bit faster because you hadn't noticed them. I looked down again, and the ants were now up to my calves and they had pretty much reached your knees. I genuinely believe if we had stood there for much more than a minute, we would have been covered head to toe!"

There's a photo in my album of one of the ants on my boot and to my incredibly untrained eye, it looks like a large leafcutter ant. This would make sense as they are more plentiful, less aggressive and don't bite unless aggravated. Having said that, their bite still hurts and is so much less fun than a swim in the Blue Hole.

After our jaguar-free expedition to the jaguar preserve, we headed off to the nearby seaside village of Hopkins. Apparently, the village is a great place to learn about the Garifuna culture. I must have missed this, as my knowledge of the Garinagu is exactly zero. My loss, I'm sure they have a rich and varied culture—no slight intended.

I don't remember much about Hopkins, and the only photo I have is one of Simon standing on the veranda of a basic thatched hut pointing into the distance. The caption reads—*Hopkins. Still no anorak hooks. No water either.*

I think that tells us everything we need to know.

Actually, not quite. Simon just reminded me we arrived in Hopkins after a very long and hot trip on the bus and the first thing we did was get into our swimming togs and leap into the ocean. Bliss, you'd think, but no.

Simon, showing off his impressive swimming skills, headed for the horizon, only to suddenly stop and look around in confusion. He describes feeling like he had a bad dose of sunburn, then realising he'd swum into a swarm of tiny jellyfish and was being stung. The condition is known locally as pica-pica but fortunately Simon didn't know this which means he yelled out "Jellyfish" instead of "Pica-pica," thus avoiding considerable confusion and allowing the rest of us to exit the water with minimal damage. Well done, that man.

You'd think I'd remember more about this picturesque seaside village, but I have a theory as to why Hopkins remains a fractured, hazy memory.

Cashew wine.

Grapes do not grow in Belize, so that restricts the wine industry somewhat. However, Belizeans are an inventive bunch and, rather than give up viticulture altogether, they turned to other fruits to make their wine.

One of the most popular libations is cashew wine. Confusingly, it's not made from the nut—that would be weird. It's made from cashew fruit, or cashew apple, as they are also known. I didn't even know this was a thing.

To make the wine, the nut is removed and then the fruit goes through a fermentation process which can take anywhere from a week to a month. The only additives are sugar, water, and yeast. Then, Bingo—a wine-like substance emerges.

Simon loved the stuff, going so far as to call it 'the best alcoholic beverage ever created,' also claiming that it should be the most popular drink in the world.

He might have had a few by then.

I don't remember being quite so enamoured, but then I don't recall much about it at all, possibly because it's incredibly strong.

Belizeans have a saying: 'Be careful (any saying that starts with 'be careful' is bound to be good). The next day, when you're in the sun, you will still be drunk.'

Other locally made wines include ginger, craboo (a native fruit that sounds totally made up), tamarind, blackberry and sorrel. We didn't try any of those, which is probably a good thing, given Simon's reaction to cashew wine.

After our trip to Hopkins, we travelled to Placencia, a small village on a long, sandy peninsula on the Southern Coast of Belize.

I was excited about this as Francis Ford Coppola has a place there and I have a screenplay I just know he'd love. Directors are thrilled when writers they don't know turn up at their holiday homes and pitch them film ideas.

Charlize, Tiger, Leonardo (not the turtle) and Harrison are also regular visitors to Placencia, so my pitching chances were high, and I also planned to get in a round or two with Woods.

Sadly, none of this happened. They were all busy. Just my luck to hit the one day they'd all mysteriously gone out of town.

Fortunately, Placencia (I keep wanting to call it Placenta, which would be a great name for a village) had other things to keep us occupied.

Are you ready for this?

Placencia holds the Guinness Book of World Records for .... the narrowest main street in the world. It was constructed nearly forty years ago, so local fishermen could wheelbarrow their fish to market without struggling through the sand. This is one of the best reasons for building a street I can think of.

I have a photo of me on the main street and I can confirm that it is, indeed, very narrow.

Aside from that and the lack of celebrities, there wasn't much else to do in Placencia. Nice, but.

Now it was time for Simon and me to say goodbye to Mary and the oldies. The official part of the tour was at an end and we headed for islands off the coast of Belize so Simon could learn to dive.

Maybe we'd see a jaguar out there. The odds were probably better than in the preserve.

CHAPTER ELEVEN

BREATHING IS OVERRATED

Belize 1997—Why are we still in Belize? Come on Glenn, get on with it.

So far, Belize had exceeded our expectations on the land. Now, it was time to see what it offered on the ocean, or rather, under it.

Having had our fill of Mayan ruins and jungle, Simon and I decided it was time to decamp to a tropical island. Simon was keen to get his PADI (Professional Association of Diving Instructors) certificate, and I was keen to do as little as humanly possible.

Finding said island wouldn't be difficult, as Belize has heaps of them. It is home to the second largest barrier reef in the world, the first being off the coast of Australia. The Belize reef is three-hundred kilometres long and contains an incredible diversity of plants and animals, including seventy hard coral species, thirty-six soft coral species, five-hundred species of fish and hundreds of invertebrates. It is a world heritage site and contains seven marine reserves.

It is also home to 450 cayes and three atolls. A caye, also spelt cay or key, is a small sandy island that is situated on top of a coral reef, which makes them perfect for ocean layabouts like myself.

The caye Simon and I visited was called Caye Caulker and is located thirty-two kilometres northeast of Belize City. Just in case you'd like to visit.

Importantly, it also had an air-strip, so we were able to fly there using the services of Tropic Air, a very small local airline with very small planes and a surprisingly good safety record. Okay, so they ran off the runway into the sea a few times. No big deal, no one's perfect. Relax.

We stayed on the runway when they flew us so they are alright with me.

For the sake of accuracy, I'm not sure if we stayed in nearby San Pedro on Caye Ambergris or Caye Caulker or both. I think both but, after a while, all those tropical paradises look the same.

Where we stayed isn't really the point. Let's just assume it was a lovely thatched hut on a sandy beach, with a pool and exotic cocktails (no cashew wine, but).

To achieve your PADI certificate, you first had to do a lot of classroom study, eight to ten hours-worth. That's where they lost me. I didn't do that at school, no way was I doing it on holiday!

Simon, however, was determined and hit the books. He did so as I lounged around the pool drinking beer. This was one of the finest decisions I have ever made and even though Simon became a certified diver and I just got slightly fatter, I'd do it again in a heartbeat.

The second stage of his dive course was a series of mini-dives with his instructors, mainly shallow dives—thirty to forty feet, with a maximum allowed depth of sixty-feet.

Remember this fact, as it becomes extremely relevant shortly.

Normally, this stage of the training would be done in a swimming pool but with hundreds of kilometres of crystal-clear ocean metres away, you'd be mad not to take advantage, so Simon only did sea dives.

Belize at this time was a haven for scuba enthusiasts. It had a plethora of incredible dive spots and the sport seemed largely unregulated. I suspect it was a bit like the wild-west for divers and instructors. No one was really watching, and as long as they didn't drown too many tourists, it was all good.

As you'd imagine, this kind of atmosphere attracted some very interesting characters. Two of which were instructing Simon. I can't remember their names, which will come as no surprise to anyone who knows me. I'm slightly dyslexic and numbers and names elude me.

Side-note: If I've met you before, please don't be offended if I have no idea what your name is. It's nothing personal (unless you're really boring). I've done it to everyone who knows me. My wife was well aware of this failing and whenever she saw me floundering, she would step in and introduce herself, thus eliciting the other person's name—God bless her. I don't think anyone was fooled by this, as I would have been unsuccessfully fishing for their moniker for quite some time by then. "Where are you working now?" was always a good way to try to figure out where I met them. This hardly ever worked because even if I ascertained their place of employment, there was no guarantee it would jog my memory name wise. I'd have been better off just being honest and saying I have the recall of a brain-damaged goldfish.

Back to the scuba instructors.

Fun fact—Belize was, and still is, the principal place used for jungle warfare training by the British Army. So, it wasn't at all surprising that one of our instructors was an ex-member of the British Special Boat Service, which is the Royal Marines equivalent of the highly impressive SAS.

The second instructor was a recently released Navy Seal, which is another elite naval fighting unit, this time from the United States.

Suffice to say, these were highly trained, incredibly competent, super-fit, hard-men. Just like the two of us, really.

Things went swimmingly (ha!) for Simon during the classroom sessions and the mini-dives. He passed with flying colours, even persuading me to come out for a splash around with his instructors. Conveniently, they gave me a temporary Learner's Day Pass to scuba with them. I learnt a few basics about the buddy system and what signals to use if you got into trouble. Apparently, thrashing around in the water like the woman in the opening sequence of Jaws isn't an official signal. What idiot thought them up? That one's a sitter.

I didn't pay that much attention. 'Pah!' I thought, 'like, I'd ever have to use those.'

The course was five days long if my memory serves me correctly and it was all leading up to Simon's big open-water dive. Technically, and probably legally, he wasn't supposed to go deeper than sixty-feet, but his instructors said they would push that as they had a great diving spot in mind and Simon had proved extremely capable.

I got on well with them both. Being an ex-cop, they felt (wrongly) that we shared a common bond of being highly trained and dedicated to the service of one's country. Completely misreading my capabilities, they invited me to join them in the open-water dive. Simon almost spat out his beer.

If I paid them a nominal fee, they'd call it a resort dive (maximum allowed depth thirty-feet) and the four of us would explore some deep-water coral caves.

Awesome. Somehow, I had avoided doing all the boring classroom crap and was getting to do the cool stuff. Score. It didn't occur to me I'd be diving at depth with minimal training and could potentially get into a life-or-death situation.

I had complete faith in the instructors. They were kick-arse dudes and knew what they were doing, right?

On the day of the dive, we were loaded into a high-powered speedboat and taken to a remote spot in the reef. It was a beautiful, clear, sunny day and the underwater visibility was superb. There were no other dive boats about.

We had the place to ourselves.

The SBS Brit anchored up, and I was teamed with the Navy Seal. He took me through the scuba diving equipment. I was put in a wetsuit and fitted with a BCD—Buoyancy Control Device, mask, regulator, single tank, fins and booties, dive weights and, most importantly, dive gauges. These would show me the depth I was at and, crucially, the amount of air I had left.

My dive-buddy had all the above, plus a dive knife, dive lights, a compass and an octopus. Not an actual, ink-squirting, eight-legged, tasty octopus—which would be cool—no, it's a spare regulator that allows a diver to share the air left in their tank in an emergency.

For non-divers, unlike myself, I'll elaborate on a couple of key pieces of equipment.

The BCD allows the diver to control their buoyancy while underwater. This permits you to stay at depth without the need to continually kick with fins, conserving energy and air.

The regulator is a breathing device which provides divers with the appropriate gas/air combo at ambient pressure so they can breathe naturally, without excessive effort, regardless of depth. The regulator has two stages; the first reduces the pressurised air from a high (300 bar) to intermediate (10 bar) pressure. The second further reduces intermediate pressure to ambient pressure for ease of breathing.

Actually, all you really need to know is that being able to breathe while underwater is quite important.

Other things to watch out for when diving include sharks (avoid) and other ocean nasties, getting snagged on shit (don't do that), getting lost (bad) and, the one most likely to get you, the bends (not the Radiohead album).

The bends or decompression sickness is a medical condition caused by emerging bubbles inside the body tissues during decompression. That doesn't sound too bad, right? Bubbles are fun. Everyone likes bubbles—insert Michael Jackson joke here.

They are less fun if they turn up uninvited in various parts of the body:

Shoulders, knees, elbows and ankles—hurty.

Lungs, brains, spinal cord—a bit deathy.

The severity of symptoms varies from barely noticeable to rapidly fatal, so a terrifyingly small amount of wriggle room there.

To avoid this highly undesirable situation, divers limit their ascent rate to about thirty-three-feet per minute, performing a series of decompression stops as they surface. This includes a safety stop ten-to-twenty-feet from the surface. The gas can also build up by doing successive deep dives, which both instructors had been doing, so they were well-aware of the dangers.

Theoretically, this shouldn't have been an issue for me, as I wasn't supposed to pass the thirty-foot mark, anyway. Not that I'd be counting. I was happy to go where the instructors took me.

Having said that, there's nothing like having an insurance policy. Simon and I decided in the case of an emergency, we'd need to surface, but knew we couldn't do it quickly. We would need to breathe out slowly and consistently until we made it back up. Neither of us thought it would be possible to exhale regularly while holding our breath for any length of time, so we decided to experiment.

One evening, under strict laboratory conditions (we hadn't had any beer), we tested our breath-holding capacity, and both managed a solid minute and a half. Stage two of this highly scientific experiment was to see how long we could last while gently exhaling the whole time. To our utter amazement, we lasted for exactly the same amount of time as our previous breath-holds. This meant we could spend a minute and a half surfacing, and our lungs wouldn't explode. Theoretically. Good to know.

On the way down, we'd also be required to equalise. For those unfamiliar with the practice, I'll go over this in more detail.

Basically, your middle ears are air spaces, sealed by the eardrum but connected to the outside by the Eustachian tubes, which run down the back of your throat. As a diver descends, water pressure bends the eardrum inwards. This is less than ideal and quite painful. To restore the volume lost to pressure, divers need to send air into the middle ear via the Eustachian tubes which will equalise or 'pop' your ears.

You can do this in a number of ways.

Most divers are taught to equalise by pinching their nose and blowing gently. This is what I do, normally not that gently. I don't do anything delicately.

You can also equalise by exhaling (the Valsalva Manoeuvre—obviously named after Antonio Maria Valsalva, the seventeenth-century physician and anatomist famous for his work with the human ear, but then you knew that) or by using your throat muscles (the Frenzel Manoeuvre—naturally named after Hermann Frenzel, the German ear nose and throat physician and Luftwaffe commander, duh, of course). Other methods of equalising include swallowing, wiggling or stretching your jaws, or swallowing while pinching your nose.

It doesn't matter which method you use, as long as you do it. Failure to equalise causes your ears to hurt while diving and potentially damages the mechanisms of the ear.

I like my ears working, so I made sure I equalised every two or three feet as recommended and had no problems with the descent.

And what a descent it was. We were guided down by the boat's anchor rope and just kept descending. Down, down, down, like a rock lobster (subtle B52's reference).

Actually, it was down, down, down, like someone who wasn't on a resort dive. I hadn't checked my depth-gauge because I was too busy taking in all the glorious sights that surrounded me.

I'm not sure of the exact location of the dive, but it was deep, and the topography of the reef allowed us to swim through coral canyons and arches that were teeming with marine life. This was a good-news, bad-news scenario.

The good news—it was an incredible diving experience.

The bad news—it was an incredible diving experience which caused me to suck in massive lungfuls of air as I marvelled at the wonders of the reef.

"ffffffffffffff, what's that over there? ffffffffffffff, was that a manta ray? ffffffffffffff, how colourful is that coral! ffffffffffffffff, This is awesome!"

This was all internal monologue, of course, and I didn't realise I was inhaling an unusual amount of tank air. No-one did, initially.

Potential life-ending disaster occurred when we approached a long and particularly narrow enclosed rock tunnel. The channel was too tight for our instructors to swim alongside, keeping an eye on us, which, to their credit, they were very diligent about doing.

The trench was about 30-40 metres long and would require a staggered formation with the SBS guy first, then Simon and me and finally, the Navy Seal.

The instructors checked all our equipment and gauges before entering the tunnel and it was fine—we both had plenty of air.

However, I went into full air-sucking over-excitement throughout the tunnel and, just as we exited, I went to draw a breath, and my mask sucked into my face.

Drawing on my minutes of diving experience, I realised something may have been wrong and waved to the Navy Seal. He swam quickly to me and grabbed my dive gauge. His eyes widened with disbelief. I was out of air.

Somehow, in the space of several minutes in the tunnel, I'd gone from plenty of air to almost completely empty.

I caught a glimpse of the depth-gauge—we were at one hundred-and-ten feet. A touch more than the allowed thirty-feet.

To summarise: I'm a wildly inexperienced diver. We are at a depth of one-hundred-and-ten feet. I have run out of air.

The Seal immediately grabbed me by the buoyancy vest and pulled me close. He said afterwards; he was worried about me panicking and tearing his mouthpiece out.

Nothing could have been further from my mind.

Despite the precariousness of the situation, I was remarkably calm. This wasn't an act of bravery. I was just too stupid to realise how much danger I was in.

I also had faith in the dive instructors. They were special-forces after all.

Once he ascertained I wasn't wigging out, he showed he was going to remove my mouthpiece and replace it with the octopus (spare regulator) that was connected to his tank. I nodded my agreement. I was pretty keen to get some air; my lungs were starting to notice something wasn't right.

The changeover went smoothly, but he still held my vest tightly. He indicated we swim over to his fellow instructor and let him know what was going on.

He showed his SBS buddy my gauge. The other instructor's eyes also widened and even though I can't read air bubbles but I'm pretty sure he said "Holy Fuck!"

He pointed to the surface, and the Seal nodded.

We swam slowly back to the anchor rope and began a gradual ascent. I made sure I kept my breathing as shallow as I could because I noticed the instructor looking at his own gauges with concern.

If we both ran out of air, we'd be screwed.

The other danger we faced was decompression sickness. We couldn't just sprint for the surface. We had to measure our ascent to ensure none of those nasty nitrogen bubbles got to treat our bodies like bouncy castles.

We stopped several times on the way back up and thankfully he had enough air left in his tank to keep us both breathing.

When we made it back to the dive boat and took off our gear, he slumped into his seat with obvious relief. He thanked me for staying calm, which wasn't really necessary, given he had just saved my life.

Simon and his instructor arrived back to the boat about half an hour later—he had plenty of air left after the tunnel (show off) and the SBS diver's relief was palpable. He made a point of congratulating his colleague on getting me back safely.

Seeing a Special Boat Service diver making a big deal of the Navy Seal's rescue drove home how precarious the situation must have been. These were elite, seasoned divers behaving as if they'd just successfully completed a high-stakes mission behind enemy lines.

Simon looked at me and just shook his head. He didn't have to say anything. He told me later that, knowing my deep attraction for doing anything that has genuine potential to cause me harm, he wasn't at all surprised.

Amazingly, they allowed me to do one more dive with Simon. I ran out of air again. No-one was shocked. It seemed, me inhaling like a hyperventilating whale was 'the new normal'.

Sadly, diving wasn't going to be my thing.

Not if I wanted to live.

Chapter PostScript from Simon:

The Diving School was very quiet while we were there. I'm not sure if it was out of season, but I don't remember many other customers being around. So, it was pretty much the two of us hanging out—me studying, you drinking beer—for the best part of a week.

During this time, I chatted with the SBS guy quite a bit. I'm not quite sure why we got on with each other, but we seemed to.

Toward the end of this period, he surprised me by sharing aspects of his experiences of the first Gulf War. It was unexpected because people who have seen genuine action in battle are usually reluctant to speak about it, especially anyone in the special-forces. Their reputation for secrecy ensures they are even less likely to talk.

One afternoon, I asked him what sort of missions he had been involved with. He said he spent most of his time behind enemy lines knocking out Scud missile sites. This was no great surprise, as it was widely reported at the time that this is what British special-forces were focussed on. He explained their role was simply to go in at night, plant explosives, and get out without being seen. This was key because if they were discovered, not only would it be a complete failure as an operation, but things were also likely to go very badly, very quickly, for them personally.

I kind of knew this already, but it was interesting to hear it confirmed by a genuine special-forces person as opposed to something I'd seen in the movies.

But it was what came next that was really unexpected.

He said. "In many ways, it was actually very easy. You go in, plant your explosives, and get out. Then you'd sit on the top of a dune, press a button and... BOOM!"

He grew very serious and continued.

"After the explosion, you'd look through your night-vision binoculars and watch burning people running around covered in green flames. That wasn't very easy at all."

This wasn't just a guy getting sentimental in his old age. He was only just into his forties and would still be one of the first called up if a similar conflict happened again. He had already told me that anyone in the special-forces had to be available for active duty until they were forty-five.

It's easy to think people in the elite units either don't have any empathy or have it drilled out of them. That they aren't bothered by what they do and see.

It was interesting to discover that even though he was a trained killing machine, he still hadn't lost his humanity.

CHAPTER TWELVE

LA STORIES

Los Angeles-multiple years. Thank God, we've moved on. The following stories have been inspired by a mixture of memories, photos, Simon's diary (again) and half written journal entries.

I've changed things up for this chapter because that's just the kind of wild and crazy guy I am. Instead of writing separately about my experiences in LA, I'm going to lump them all together in a series of anecdotes about the city—the good, the bad and the ugly—which, annoyingly, wasn't shot in LA because that would have been a great segue.

Don't like that idea? Tough. It's my book.

I've been to LA many times over many years, mainly because my lovely wife used to travel twice a year for her work as a buyer and merchandise manager. LA was her first buying stop, and then it was on to London. I often accompanied her on these trips because, well, why wouldn't you? The accommodation was paid for by the company, so I only needed to cover flights and food. Score. I also hated it when my wife was away, so any excuse to be with her was grabbed with both hands.

It would be logical to start with one of the trips I shared with her or the first trip I ever made to LA but, as I said, that would be logical, so I won't be doing that.

Instead, I'm going to do a highlights package of the time Simon and I had in LA on our way back from Belize, so it sorta flows on from the last chapter, but really because it's fresh in my mind.

The thing that stands out most from Simon and my trip is The Viper Room—a legendary LA Hotspot, owned at the time by Johnny Dep. The nightclub has something of a chequered history, being the scene of actor River Phoenix's death from a drug overdose in the year it opened. Australian singer and actor Jason Donovan also suffered a drug-induced seizure at the club but survived. Musician, and all round bad girl Courtney Love, followed suit by overdosing there as well. Depp performed CPR and saved her life.

It was known as a hangout for Hollywood's aspiring actors and beautiful people, so Simon and I would fit right in. Or maybe not, given we'd packed mainly for the jungle. I found a pair of jeans that had seen better days, though once I'd scraped the Tapir pooh off, they were fine. In fact, I may have started a trend. Hard to tell in LA.

We arrived at the club and, surprisingly, were given entry.

It was a weeknight. I'm sure that helped.

It was also a twenties' themed evening, and the place was filled with couples dressed as if they'd just come out of a speakeasy. They looked fabulous—all vintage inspired twirly skirts, blouses, shirts and pants, but with a modern twist, as most of the dancers were heavily tattooed.

Simon and I did NOT fit right in.

A fantastic swing band started up and the moment the first notes pulsed, the crowd moved as one to the dance floor. I'm buggered if I know what was going on, but it seemed like every couple there were professional dancers. Maybe they were all from a swing dancing club or it was audition night for Soul Train? The only thing we were sure of was that Simon and I were terrified someone would ask us to dance.

I don't dance. So, that's not strictly true. I do dance, I just don't do it well. I have very little sense of rhythm and for many years, instead of timing my movements to drum or bass, I moved in time to the lead guitar. This made me look like I'd escaped from a special needs class and had received an electric shock on the dance floor while standing on a banana peel. The only person who would voluntarily dance with me was my long-suffering wife.

Fortunately, our jungle chic look put off any possible dance partners, and we were free to relax and observe.

The thing that fascinated both of us most was a couple who were sitting at a table next to ours. From the moment they arrived, until the moment they left, they were at each other's throats. This wasn't just a disagreement, this was a completely unashamed full-on blazing row. I've seen cats and dogs with friendlier relationships.

It wasn't the intensity of the fighting that was truly surprising. Every ten minutes or so, when the band struck up a new song, they would pause their arguing, get up on the dance floor, and dance together in total harmony. They were easily the best dancers there, which is saying something given the calibre of every other dancer in the joint. It was something to behold; they didn't miss a beat, twirling and jiving in perfect sync with each other. Then, the moment the song stopped, they were at each other's throats again. Back to their table, bicker, bicker, bicker—new song, BANG! King and Queen of the dance floor.

It was one of the strangest relationships I had ever seen.

We got through the evening without our lack of dance skills being exposed or of us dying of a drug overdose, so we counted that as a win.

According to my photo album, we spent the rest of our time in LA going to a family restaurant called Hooters. The servers were very friendly if I remember correctly—can't recall what the food was like.

For reasons that escape me, we also hit all the fashion brand shops on Rodeo Drive in Beverly Hills. We were either getting our partners nice gifts (most likely) or upping our act, fashion-wise (Simon—already pretty stylish—Me, nah).

Once we'd tired of shopping—about three minutes—we went to Universal Studios. This was much more my speed. I'm a massive movie fan. I tell people it's because I'm a screenwriter. While there is some correlation, that's not strictly true. I'd adore movies even if I wasn't trying to write them.

I loved Universal Studios and have been there many times over a variety of visits. I'm going to lump them all together and give you a snapshot of my impressions and favourite rides/attractions. You can trust my advice—I'm a comedy writer.

Old school and probably not available any more—*Backdraft*. I have an admission to make. I like fire. I like everything about it (except for getting burnt). I like the way it looks; I like the way it smells. I like its comforting warmth and romantic properties. There's nothing more satisfying than starting a fire, especially one that's difficult to ignite. With a few less morals, I'd definitely be a pyromaniac. As it is, I'm skirting the edge. So, yeah, I was always going to like anything that involved flames. It would probably look hokey now, but it stood out to me at the time.

The only thing I like better than fire is explosions, particularly fiery ones, so naturally the Waterworld show was going to be number one on my list. I sit firmly within the controversial camp that loved the movie. Dennis Hopper chewed scenery. We saw Jeanne Tripplehorn's bum, Kevon Costner had gills and lots of stuff blew up—what's not to like?

The Universal Studios show didn't fail to deliver. It's the number one rated attraction in the park and over the course of a year there are approximately 168,500 pyrotechnic effects, including giant fireballs rising fifty feet in the air! Let me just repeat that—GIANT FIREBALLS. You'd have to be dead inside not to enjoy that. Simon and I loved every mad minute.

How do you beat giant fireballs? Well, you don't, but a dinosaur-themed log flume comes pretty bloody close. That's right, it's the *Jurassic Park* ride.

Allsortofsaurus's appeared from behind trees and rocks, burst from pools and generally scared the bejesus out of anyone under the age of ten (and Simon—naturally, I was cool). And, at the end, we hurtled down a cliff into a dinosaur filled lake, creating a massive splash and soaking anyone who wasn't paying attention (and some who were).

Note to idiots. If you're going on a log flume ride, there is a better-than-average chance that you will get wet. When this happens, don't look surprised and grumble about your track pants getting a bit of water on them.

The next attraction isn't a ride, per se, but is a must do. It's the Universal Studios world famous Studio Tour, and it's pretty bloody good. Thinking about it, *Backdraft* might have been part of that, but let's not quibble.

The things I remember most about the tour were:

Crappy jokes from the host/voice over. Essential on almost any excursion of note.

The 'scare' from the *Jaws* shark, whilst passing through Amity Island. I've got a bridge to sell anyone who didn't see that coming.

Note: Spielberg called the shark Bruce after his accountant. Excellent.

Another note: The shark was even crappier than you might imagine, which just makes the movie even more impressive in my view. Anyone who can make a dodgy fake shark as terrifying as Spielberg did deserves a massive amount of credit. Although I still haven't forgiven him for making the vast majority of my surf sessions a distressing affair.

Another Spielberg stunner. The smouldering wreckage of a Boeing 747 from *the War of the Worlds*. Regardless of what you thought of the film, this set was hugely impressive. The amount of detail was mind-boggling. You really felt like you were driving through the devastation caused by a real plane crash. Hat's off.

These days they've added a *Fast and Furious* event and a *King Kong* 3D experience created by Peter Jackson, so I imagine those would be very cool.

Harry Potter also seems to make a plethora of appearances at the park. It's bound to be well done given the rabid passion of the fans, but this is pure supposition on my part.

If you're in LA, go to Universal Studios. Unless you are a track suit wearing, fun-hating, buzz-killer. In that case, stay home.

My best day in Los Angeles, aside from precious memories of

travelling with my wife, occurred when I fulfilled a lifelong dream—surfing a Malibu longboard at Malibu beach.

You can call me out on hyperbole there. My lifelong desire is to see a moose in the wild. My wish to jump on a log at the famous surf-break isn't that old. In fact, it was probably only born twenty years ago, when I started surfing in any serious way.

I grew up in New Plymouth, New Zealand, with some of the best surf-breaks in the country on my doorstep. The famous surf highway was a stone's throw from me and yet, all those amazing waves remained unridden by me. There were several very good reasons for that.

First, surfing was a relatively unknown sport when I was a boy and those that did it were seen as hippies or rebels—as opposed to future pillars of the community like my good self. I had a mate who surfed, and I thought he was mad, especially as he returned from a session one day and reported that the front of his board had been chomped by a shark. Or so he said. This particular mate was famous for exaggeration, so we never found out the truth. Just the thought of tangling with a Great White was enough to put me off.

Second, I had the balance and grace of a drunk sloth. Klutz, kook, jinx, Gonzo. All words that could be (and often were) applied to me as a young man. There's some evidence they still apply. Anyone reading this book won't find that hard to believe. As a young man, I had one attempt at surfing, jumping on a ten-foot board at a local beach. I wasn't terrible, but I wouldn't threaten the world tour either. It also didn't really capture me at the time.

I'd grown up around the ocean and had always loved waves. This was pre-boogie-boards, but we still took on ridiculously large swells as body-surfers or on cheap polystyrene lie-down boards. We were often pulverised by the surf, but we were young, so bounced back quickly.

Surfing didn't really get a grip on me until my early forties, then it grabbed me like a possessed octopus and never let go. Once I'd experienced the thrill of speeding along the face of a big, clean wave on a summer's day; that was it. I was gone.

Bearing all this in mind, the chance to surf Malibu was too much to turn down. It's an iconic location for surfers made famous as the spot Kathy Kohner aka 'Gidget' surfed in the 1959 movie. It's known for having a south facing shoreline that attracts a perfect, peeling wave, stacked to the horizon and the crowds that go with such conditions.

I went there (the first time) on a small, sunny day with clean one to two footers rolling through, but not enough grunt to attract a lot of people. I hired a nine-foot board from the Malibu Surf Shack just across the road from the surf break—or at least it used to be, it's permanently closed now which I'm assuming makes my T-shirt and sticker all the more valuable.

I crossed the main highway without dying, which was more difficult than one would have thought, hit the beach and paddled out.

My main memory of the session is sitting on the board out the back of the break, waiting for a wave when a squadron of pelicans (correct term, I think you'll find) flew past me, almost skimming the water. The sun was shining; the water was clear and warm. It was such a perfect Southern California moment.

Minutes later, a decent sized swell came out of nowhere and reared up. It was the best wave of the day and I was in exactly the right spot. I leapt to my feet and got in front of a clean, curving wall of deep green water, staying right in the curl the whole way to the beach. A long ride with the only troubling moment occurring as I dismounted in the middle of some shallow rocks. At any other time, I'd have hit them, but not that day.

It was an excellent ride, and I surfaced to find an old surfer had come down from the beach to see me.

"Great wave, dude", he said with a huge grin on his face.

I acknowledged the compliment and told him it was my first time surfing there.

He clapped me on the shoulder and said, "Well, brother, you can say you've really surfed Malibu."

I believe the correct term for how I felt is 'stoked'.

It seems I have underestimated just how many LA Stories I have. Certainly enough for another chapter, so keep reading for my worst day, most embarrassing moment and more...

CHAPTER THIRTEEN

LOST ANGELES

Los Angeles-multiple years. Much to my amazement (and probably yours) I found a completed diary chronicling my adventures at Pitchfest (keep reading). My daughter also diarised her Hollywood adventures. The rest are unreliable recollections.

My worst day in the Big Apple was considerably less fun than my best.

In a fit of what can only be called madness, I hired a car and drive out to a nature trail to go for a walk. The trail I'd selected promised the possibility of wildlife spotting, including coyotes, foxes, skunks, lizards, squirrels, and then, in very small print, rattlesnakes.

What should have occurred to me (but didn't) was all of these things live in the desert. Had I realised this, I probably would have reconsidered attempting the walk in forty-degree heat and maybe, just maybe, I would have taken more water with me than the small bottle I got out of the hotel mini-bar fridge. Thinking back, I don't believe it was even full.

Coming from New Zealand, it's virtually impossible not to have been on at least a few tramps. Actually, I think it's compulsory. You can't call yourself a Kiwi unless you've trudged along a few bush tracks and marvelled at a mountain or two. Which is to say, I was a reasonably experienced tramper and should have known better than to go to an unknown track woefully unprepared.

Driving through the LA streets and on the freeways was as harrowing as always, especially for those of us who normally drive on the left.

Pro tip: As long as you keep the centre line beside your driver's-side window and don't crash into a multi-million-dollar supercar, you'll be okay.

I arrived at the starting point of the track, flustered but with no lawsuits pending, chucked on a backpack holding a rain jacket (ha!), a small energy bar, and my pathetic bottle of water, then headed off.

The trail itself was hot, dusty, and devoid of anything. And I mean anything. No people, fauna, interesting sights, markers, water sources, shade, or identifying features. I'd describe the landscape as sparse, scrubby and desolate. Just what you want from a scenic walk.

It was also surprisingly hilly. And hot. Did I mention the heat? I don't think I can overstate just how scorching it was. I wisely headed out mid-afternoon, unquestionably the hottest part of the day.

After about an hour of stumbling around, wondering exactly where the rattlesnakes were hiding, I realised I was almost out of water. This would have been a good time to go back, but I'd seen a grove of trees ahead and thought they might be hiding something interesting. They weren't.

I found a bit of shade and was able to bring my core temperature down from boiling to merely overheated.

As I drained the last of my water, it finally dawned on me I should return to the car park.

Was it the left trail or the right? Left. I'm certain.

I was less certain half an hour later when looped back to the trees.

It was just one great decision after another.

I was in serious trouble now. My water was gone, I was dehydrated, had no energy, the sun was unrelenting, and I was still a long way from the car-park.

At this point, a Lycra'd-up fitness mum turned up. She was pushing a baby in one of those mountain buggy strollers. Unlike me, she was completely prepared for the weather. The stroller was shaded—she wore a hat and appeared effectively hydrated.

She asked if I was all right. I did the stupid male thing and said I was. This was clearly a lie, and she knew it. She offered me a swig of water. I'm dumb, but I'm not suicidal. I nodded my thanks and took a sip. I wanted to glug the whole bottle but that would have been rude so I practiced restraint.

She offered me more. I said I was fine. She looked at me dubiously but decided not to argue with the mad Kiwi and then my Lululemon-clad angel was gone.

It's no exaggeration to say that swig of water probably saved my life.

By the time I made it back to the car-park I was staggering, not walking. I was desiccated, my vision swam, my parched brain on the verge of hallucination. I had nothing left. I needed water, and I needed it fast. There were no shops around but there was a small office complex close to the carpark. I dragged my ravaged body into the building. The receptionist took one look at me and literally ran to the water cooler and began pouring me cups of water. At one point, I was lying under the tap.

Once I'd recovered sufficiently, I thanked the receptionist profusely, rejecting her offer to get me medical assistance, went to the toilet and threw up. Only a small amount, though. Nothing to see here.

Once I got back in the car, I went straight to a 7-Eleven and bought a vat of Powerade to get my electrolytes back to pre-near-death levels.

Upon returning to the hotel, I told Eula of my adventures, not because I liked to torment my wife (though this was usually the end result), but because I wanted sympathy. I got a lecture (deserved), scolding (deserved), incredulous comments on my stupidity (deserved), and finally compassion (undeserved).

. . .

Righto, let's delve straight into my most embarrassing Los Angeles experience. Fun.

My daughter Devon is an extremely talented girl. Obviously, she takes after her mother. When she was sixteen she auditioned for, and got the part of, Brenda Aarons in the movie *Bridge to Terabithia*. The film was being shot in New Zealand and her character was a sister to the main lead, Jesse Aarons, played by Josh Hutcherson. The movie also starred AnnaSophia Robb, Zooey Deschanel and Robert Patrick (the cyborg cop from Terminator 2).

No prizes for guessing who I was most excited to meet.

The director was Gabor Csupo, who is known for his animation work as the creator of *Rugrats, Duckman, The Wild Thornberrys* and more.

Once the movie was completed, we were invited to the premiere at the El Capitan Theatre on Hollywood boulevard on February 3rd, 2007.

Hollywood premiere? Yes, please. It was never going to happen for me, so the least I could do was hold on to my daughter's coat-tails.

My wife was working, so it would just be my daughter and me attending. Plus a sizeable contingent of New Zealand parents and kids who had various parts in the movie. There was quite a buzz around the premiere, especially among the Kiwi crew, and several of the kids were also auditioning for pilot season or looking to get agents. Devon wasn't interested in all that, but she was excited to walk the red carpet on the big day.

She had her outfit picked out. A stunning red dress and black jacket. This was completed by a large white handbag. I went all in black, not a suit (I don't do suits) but tidy trousers and a collared shirt, which is a big change from my usual jeans and t-shirt. One must make an effort for big occasions.

Come the day and the paparazzi were out in force. AnnaSophia, Josh and Zooey were already stars in their own right and Hayden Panettiere had done a song for the film, so was also on the red carpet. Devon and the Kiwi kids had their photos taken and stars sauntered by. I stood in the background with one of the other dads and took it all in. Insanely proud of my daughter.

As the fuss reached its zenith, Devon waved me over. She was about to be interviewed about her role in the film and wanted me to hold her handbag while she talked.

I did what any dutiful dad would have done and slung her bag over my shoulder, even though it clashed terribly with my outfit.

I didn't realise I had accidentally walked behind some of the other stars as they were being interviewed, so there's some very funny footage of me strolling along the red carpet with a large, white, woman's handbag over my shoulder.

I'd like to think I was being very fashion forward and pushing gender boundaries, but we all know the truth.

That evening, we went to the director's house in Beverly Hills. He'd built it around a ten-seat cinema in the basement. A rocket-ship crashed through one of the lounge walls and a sculpture of a giant shark came through the floor. His swimming pool had purvey viewing bubbles in it and the stairs to the upper-stories were accompanied by fish tanks full of turtles. The walls were lined with paintings by Matisse, Renoir, Dali, and Picasso. I'm pretty sure they weren't copies.

Taking all this in, I turned to Devon and said, "How cool is this?"

She looked at me and said, "Yeah, Dad, but none of it's real." She was sixteen at the time.

That's my girl.

Now for some classic LA moments and impressions—this will cover multiple trips.

When Devon and I were there, we started a tradition of counting how many persons of dubious mental clarity we'd seen. The record was twenty-two in one trip, including one guy dressed as Jesus walking along the middle of the motorway, yelling at cars.

Eula always stayed at the Luxe Hotel near Rodeo Drive when she was working in LA. This allowed her and her team to be close to the main shopping areas so they could buy samples for work.

The Luxe was a very nice hotel, and I loved being amongst the glitz and glamour of the area, watching the beautiful people come and go and shooting off on solo day trips to explore the city.

You'd think I'd feel guilty about lounging around, enjoying myself while Eula was working, but you'd be wrong. She adored her job and loved having me with her when she travelled, so everyone was happy.

My main impressions of the patrons and staff of the Luxe are as follows:

Staff—aspiring actors, screenwriters, directors.

Patrons—women in their sixties dressed like they were in their thirties, with faces and bodies that wouldn't have moved in a hurricane. Old men with unnaturally black hair. Possible mobsters.

Top-shelf people watching. I loved it.

I went to LA twice for work of my own. At the time, I was trying my hand at screenwriting and had pitched several movie ideas to a Hollywood producer I knew. He liked one of them (but not enough to actually pay me to write it) and I'd developed a first draft of a screenplay.

He wasn't that taken with it but still liked the idea, so I enrolled in a screenwriting course with an industry luminary by the name of Steve Kaplan. He is acknowledged as one of the leading experts in the dark art of comedy writing and has run hundreds of courses on the subject. I knew bugger all, so figured it couldn't hurt to attend and might possibly be a tax write-off. The Inland Revenue didn't agree.

The course was great, and I learned a lot—most of which I've subsequently forgotten. I never got the screenplay right though—issues with tone. All was not lost. Steve's course ignited my desire to do more screenwriting and was the catalyst for my second visit to Los Angeles.

I attended The Great American Pitch Fest.

"What's that?" I hear you ask.

Well, that depends on your point of view. It's either an unmissable opportunity to get your work in front of dozens of Hollywood heavyweights or a complete con designed to take money off desperate and largely untalented wannabes.

I know which way I'm leaning. If nothing else, it was an experience.

Prior to the event (and after you've paid the fee) you are given a list of the companies that would be attending so you can plan who you want to talk to. The festival was like speed-dating for writers. You were given five minutes to pitch your idea to your chosen production company executives, and they had the option to extend that time if they deemed you worthy.

The event itself was held in a boring, blue-collar suburb, not even remotely close to the hub of the movie industry. The building seemed to be selected for its aircraft-hangar like capacity rather than any Hollywood glitz.

Inside, the warehouse was sectioned off into seating areas for 'the powerful ones' and lines for the plebs to queue. Space had been made around the outside for a clutch of self-professed 'experts' to sell their dubious wares.

Dialling back the cynicism for a second, I will say there were some genuine and interesting people at Pitchfest. Many of them ran free courses and had real insights into the industry.

I met Blake Snyder there, the successful screenwriter of *Stop! Or My Mom Will Shoot*, and author of the brilliant screenwriting book *Save the Cat*. He was amazing. A real highlight of the festival for me and someone I stayed in contact with until his untimely death in 2009. A sincerely nice and talented man.

His valuable services stood in stark contrast to other vendors, such as the business offering to laminate your one-page synopsis for large sums of money. If your idea is shit, then all laminating it does is turn it into shiny shit.

Back to the event itself. I realised pretty quickly there wasn't any point getting in the queues for Disney or Warner Brothers. The lines were staggeringly long, and the scuttlebutt was that they sent low-level execs who had no decision-making power at all.

Instead, I focussed on smaller production companies with a few successful movies to their name and probably co-pro deals with bigger firms.

I was pitching three movie ideas (two of which were completed screenplays—if such a thing exists). As one of them is still under option, I won't reveal the plot, but the other two were a sports comedy and a police thriller.

I was optimistically targeting twenty-one companies or individual producers during the day, but in reality, I only pitched to fifteen.

The atmosphere at the event was frantic, and there was an excited buzz in the air. I couldn't help but notice there were quite a few people dressed up to pitch. I saw several angels and fairies and assume they were trying to grab people's attention. All well and good, but once you've been seen, you still need something to sell.

My strategy was not to dress up like a dick and just have good ideas. Call me crazy.

I remember three pitches going well, but probably my best opportunity came late in the day when the pitching was officially over and small groups were sitting around chatting. One of the people I was talking to was a producer for a company called Neo Art & Logic. I hadn't pitched them because I assumed they produced either animated or effects-heavy scripts which mine weren't. The producer seemed annoyed that I'd put them in that box and said they produced a wide range of movies. He insisted I pitch him something on the spot, so I told him about the sports comedy. He said he was interested, gave me his card and said to send him the screenplay.

At the end of the day, I had nine companies to email for further discussions. According to other writers I spoke to, this was a fantastic hit rate, but who knows.

As they say; 'In LA It's impossible to have a bad meeting'. Producers won't say they aren't interested, you just never hear anything back. This turned out to be the case.

Of the nine companies I contacted, four didn't respond, three requested screenplays and two gave me good feedback but didn't want to see anything further.

Ironically, only Neo Art & Logic showed any real promise with the producer's assistant loving the screenplay, but the big man himself not so keen. I was told by one producer that if I moved to LA, I could probably get a job as a studio writer, but I didn't want to do that.

All in all, it was fun and exciting but ultimately, a waste of time —which sums up Hollywood for me perfectly.

CHAPTER FOURTEEN

MONKEY BOY

Sarawak Borneo 1999. Once again we are in lost diary territory. I kept a journal of my adventures in Borneo with the express intention of writing a book about the trip. That diary has gone the way of a lot of the rainforest, lost forever. Fortunately, I'm still in touch with most of the Borneo Five and their recollections helped form the following chapters.

A week before we left for our trip to Borneo, tribal war broke out.

Awesome.

After the news emerged, the first four phone calls I received were from my travelling companions wanting to extend our stay. The next was from my mum, whom apparently I was killing with worry. The bravado of my companions was understandable. The fighting was in the Southern Indonesian half of Borneo, known as Kalimantan. Our trip would only take in the Northern Malaysian states of Sabah and Sarawak. We should be completely safe, well, not completely. This was still a largely undeveloped destination, and we were distressingly unprepared for what lay ahead.

I'd selected Borneo as a destination because it contained some of the world's last untouched tracts of rain forest and a wide diversity of flora and fauna. This appealed to my 'see it before it gets fucked up' mind-set.

All I needed now was a crew for the adventure. My wife wisely declined citing the lack of shopping malls, so I asked some friends. To my utter amazement, four agreed to join me, solely because Borneo was where 'The Wild Man' came from. This gives you a small insight into the quality of my mates.

Team Borneo was as follows; Myself at thirty-seven, the old married guy of the group, Seth, a television producer in his mid-twenties, Nguyen, an art director also in his mid-twenties, Pema, a media buyer and the youngest member of the party at twenty-one, and Struan, a thirty-one-year-old retail manager.

Note that none of these professions requires a lot of bushcraft or jungle survival experience. Bizarrely, our complete absence of any useful skills didn't deter us in the least. It should have.

With the group organised, we began our jungle training. This intensive program consisted of eating Malaysian takeaways, reading an SAS survival guide and going on three rushed tramps in the extremely un-jungle-like Waitakere Ranges in Auckland, New Zealand. Oh, and Seth bought a whistle.

Further preparations included Nguyen, for motivations known only to himself, having a pre-trip circumcision (let's not dwell on that) and Struan and I getting 'adventure haircuts'. Struans involved peroxiding his normally dark hair to a shocking yellow that frightened small children. I went further still. The best way to describe it is a reverse Mohawk. My head was completely shaved except for two purple strips of hair on either side of the centre, like racing stripes. It wasn't so much a haircut as a massacre, though to be fair to the stylist, the lines were impressively straight. My wife and Struan's partner had been understandably nervous about the trip, but once they saw our haircuts, they were suddenly very keen for us to leave the country.

Fair call. We looked stupid.

Thus prepared, we flew from the safety of home to conquer the untamed wilds of Borneo.

The five of us landed in Sarawak's capital city, Kuching, and as we approached Malaysian customs, I doubted the wisdom of my new look. I was certain I'd be searched, but we were waved straight through. I guess they figured you'd have to be an incredibly stupid smuggler to draw that much attention to yourself.

Kuching, which we insisted on pronouncing as KAching, is a port city in the North of the country that sits on the Sarawak River. It's a fascinating place full of ornate Chinese temples, colonial architecture, narrow winding streets and cat statues. A lot of cat statues. I assume this was because Kuching means cat in Malay, although the city wasn't named after felines, but rather the *mata Kuching* or cat's-eye fruit that grows nearby.

Lining the streets were rows and rows of shops and market stalls containing all sorts of exotic food and paraphernalia. The sights and smells were incredible; brightly coloured fruits, vegetables and spices sat on a maze of stalls and street vendors tended charcoal fires which spat fat and flame at anyone who walked too close. It was so culturally different and exciting that jet lag was soon forgotten and we wandered around in an excited daze.

The highlight for me was the fish market. It was weird and wonderful. I've never seen such an array of fish. There are some frigging strange things in the ocean, or, as was the case, currently out of it and being displayed on top of old tile benches.

Blunt-nosed, big-eyed striped tropical fish sat beside long, skinny eel-like creatures with crooked mouths curled into a snarl. Next to them sat bright red fish that came out of the ocean looking like they'd already been cooked and fat, almost translucent fish that were covered in black spots, as if they'd been attacked by a maniac with a sharpie. There were some ugly assed fish on those benches. It was great; I loved it. The fish market also seemed to like me. The stallholders were fascinated by my haircut and, once they'd established I wasn't a maniac, there was lots of friendly chatter and haircut patting.

We made it to our hotel later that day on a high. It was a nice place and the only accommodation we'd pre-booked, deciding we would have more of an adventure if we weren't on a pre-arranged schedule.

We'd visited the Semenggoh Wildlife reserve the next day, hoping to see an orangutan. The park was situated just twenty kilometres south of Kuching and we had booked a van to take us, leaving mid-morning.

As we didn't have an early start, we went to the hotel bar for a quiet drink. Before long, we were joined by a young German tourist. He was an intense, overly boisterous chap who immediately bought us beer. Our new friend downed his drink quickly, obviously up for a big night. We weren't and didn't attempt to keep up with him.

After his third pint, he announced he knew a great drinking game we could play. It was called the flaming asshole, and it involved wedging a long strip of toilet paper between your bum cheeks and setting it on fire. The goal then being to scull your drink and put out the paper before you incinerated your nether regions.

Maybe it's a cultural thing, but this sounded like the worst game in the history of the world. None of us had the remotest desire to have a wad of flaming paper wedged anywhere and certainly not there! (I don't use exclamation marks lightly, but I feel it's called for here). We politely declined, but he was determined to convince us it was a great game. He took off to the toilet and returned shortly after with a length of paper hanging from his undies. He told us to light it. Maybe German toilet paper is thicker than Malaysian, I don't know.

All I can tell you is the stuff in that hotel burned hot and fast. I think my brain has protected me from the images that followed because my memory of what happened is foggy. I remember fire, the smell of burnt hair and screaming. Lots of screaming. While we came out of that bar with mental scars, I suspect his were physical and significantly worse.

Crazy bugger.

Before heading to the wildlife reserve, we needed to find a new, cheaper hotel, preferably one without testicle-incinerating Germans. In honour of him, and because we thought the name was hilarious, we moved into the FARTA Hotel. So mature.

Once our gear was stowed, we hopped into a van and headed for Semenggoh. We were very excited. With 653 hectares of forest, the wildlife reserve is by far the biggest orangutan rehabilitation centre in Sarawak. It was established as a sanctuary in 1975 for orangutans who were injured, orphaned or kept captive as illegal pets. The centre was said to have a thriving population of captive and semi-wild adolescent and young adult orangutans who lived in the jungle reserve and visited the sanctuary for feeding.

It is also the habitat for a variety of other wildlife, including gibbons, giant and pygmy squirrels and a wide variety of birds. I'm a big fan of gibbons; squirrels and birds I can take or leave. I'm certainly not a twitcher, so a bird has to be exotic or fierce to get me interested. Eagles, vultures and toucan yes please, garden variety sparrows and tits, nah.

Orangutan, on the other hand, were in a completely different league. There was no denying their coolness factor. They are super smart, very strong, frigging huge, with adult males reaching 1.4 metres tall and weighing over 100 kilograms. That's a lot of monkey. Orangutan are also human's closest relatives sharing ninety-seven per cent of our DNA. Plus, they were movie stars; featured in such classic cinema as Planet of the Apes and the Clint Eastwood films *Every Which Way but Loose* and *Any Which Way You Can*.

I can think of no higher praise.

The van driver dropped us at the entrance to the park and we were told we would have to walk about three kilometres to the actual rehabilitation centre. He said it was a nice walk, as we'd have jungle on either side of the trail. This was correct, and we enjoyed a pleasant mini-hike along a wide and well-cleared track to get to the research centre and attractions.

Upon arrival, I remember being underwhelmed by the appearance of the buildings. It was a pretty basic set-up, but we weren't there to see a flash research centre. We were there for one thing—orangutan. And we were in luck. In the trees near a viewing platform were several of the big orange fellas and fellesses. There was a large male with long shaggy fur and an impressive flanged face, plus several much gentler-looking females with skull-shaped heads and hugely expressive eyes. They were only about fifteen to twenty metres away, so we were able to get a good look at these highly impressive creatures.

They moved through the trees with grace, hanging easily from ropes and branches by their long limbs and dexterous feet and hands. One of the females had a baby with her and the cute little guy (or girl) stayed snuggled up to mum.

The orangutan seemed very comfortable with our presence, not overly curious, but not shying away, either. We spent several hours observing them and then wandered around the rehabilitation centre, chatting with the staff and soaking up the jungle vibe. It was a brilliant visit, and we were fizzing from our sightings. Little did we know, this was just the beginning.

We left the sanctuary mid-afternoon to begin the long walk to the main road. It was hot and dry, and the return hike seemed much longer than the walk in. About three-quarters of the way back, we noticed an orangutan high in the trees beside us. He seemed to be tracking our movements and was following us in the tree line. We watched him for a few minutes, then he disappeared. Excited by another sighting, we waited to see if we could spot him again. Having no luck, we carried on along the track. We walked around a sharp bend and, to our surprise, saw an adolescent orangutan standing right in the middle of the road.

It was the same monkey who had been following us in the canopy. He was about a metre tall, lean and rangy. Without pausing, he walked straight up to me, put his hand on my shoulder and climbed up onto my chest, putting one arm around my neck. I had no idea what to do. It was an incredible moment, but I could feel the strength in his body and worried about what he might do next. I was equally awestruck and freaked out. The orangutan wasn't threatening me, but I was acutely aware it was a wild animal and anything could happen.

The rest of the boys were astounded.

"Holy shit," I exclaimed, "What do I do now?"

"Don't annoy it," Struan suggested.

"No kidding. What annoys orangutan?" I asked.

"Perhaps, don't mention Clint Eastwood," said Nguyen helpfully.

As I stood there, the orangutan pulled the collar of my tee shirt out, looked at my chest, then quickly checked out my pockets. I was wearing a belt that held drink bottles in cup-like pouches and it searched that as well, flicking the lids off the bottles with incredible dexterity. It was like being frisked by the world's hairiest pickpocket.

I assume he was looking for food, but maybe he was just curious. Even though the orangutan was supporting a lot of his own weight, he was still quite heavy, probably weighing forty to fifty kilos, and he smelled like a combination of jungle foliage and wet dog.

Once he'd finished checking my clothing, he settled into my chest and just sat there for a few minutes, quite relaxed but also keeping a close eye on what the other guys were doing. After about ten minutes, he unwound his arm from my shoulders and lowered himself to the ground. I was absolutely elated; it was easily my best-ever wildlife encounter, but I must admit to a sense of relief when he climbed down. I was acutely aware that he had been in complete control the whole time. The experience was on his terms and there was nothing I could have done had he turned feral.

As the orangutan edged away, I could see that the others were both stoked for me and also a little envious. They were keen to have a similar experience, and this quickly became a case of be careful what you wish for. I was ready to keep walking towards the exit, but several of the team wanted to see what the orangutan would do next.

I completely understood this, as I had been very lucky with my encounter, but felt we were pushing our luck by hanging around. As if in answer to my thoughts, the orangutan homed in on Pema, the youngest of our crew. It walked over to him and climbed onto his chest, similar to what it had done to me, except it went under Pema's tee-shirt so its hairy hide was directly on his skin.

At first, Pema was over the moon. The orangutan had both arms around his neck in an embrace and had snuggled up to him. It was very cute, but as time ticked by, it became clear the monkey had no intention of leaving its comfortable spot.

"Ok," Pema said to his new mate. "You can get down now."

The orangutan ignored him and then, to everyone's horror/amusement, thrust its hips in a sexual manner against Pema's chest.

"I think he likes you," suggested Struan, barely able to keep the smile from his face.

Pema began freaking out. “Get him off me,” he yelled.

“How do we do that?” replied Seth. “Orangutan have the strength of ten men...” He looked around, then continued. “And there are only four of us."

His maths was correct. There was little we could do.

The more Pema struggled, the tighter the orangutan clung to him. It was also making barking sounds. Things were getting serious.

Someone suggested we walk back to the rehabilitation centre, as the keepers would know what to do. This made sense and we turned around and headed back the way we'd come. The orangutan seemed quite happy to stay where he was, but the same couldn't be said for Pema.

“It stinks and its skin is really scratchy,” he moaned. “And what if it bites me?”

“We'd probably have to give the poor little guy antibiotics,” I said, attempting to lighten the mood. Pema glared at me.

At this point, Seth pulled a large Swiss Army knife out of his pocket and extended the biggest blade. There was an uproar from the boys.

“Whoa, Seth, what the hell! We're not stabbing it.”

We were all surprised by his action. Seth was the member of the group with the most pacifist/hippy leanings. He had long, flowing hair and an air of calm about him. Opening the knife was completely out of character.

“Chill out,” said Seth. “I'm not suggesting attacking it. I thought we could cut Pema's T-shirt off if we had to."

It was an extremely sensible suggestion and more like the Seth we knew. We all calmed down and set off again.

As we walked, I was directly behind Pema and the orangutan suddenly reached out with one of its incredibly long arms and grabbed the front of my t-shirt. He pulled me towards him and I lurched forward. The strength in its grip was astonishing. I was powerless, unable to stop myself from being dragged in his direction.

Fortunately, he let me go quite quickly but, at that moment, I knew for certain there was no way we could remove him by force, not without suffering serious injuries. Aside from the thrusting movements, which, much to Pema's horror, occurred quite frequently, the orangutan remained calm and seemed to enjoy the ride.

Finally, we arrived back at the wildlife centre. We were knackered now, especially Pema, whose chest was being rubbed raw by the coarse skin of the monkey. We called out to the keepers, and they ran over to see what the fuss was about. They were astounded. The orangutan normally kept their distance from humans, and this was incredibly unusual. They identified him as a young male who had been looked after at the centre when he was small. He had disappeared into the jungle several years ago and had been living wild ever since.

We asked how they were going to get it off Pema. They suggested hitting it with a tree branch. What the hell! We could have done that (not that we would have). It didn't seem like a particularly scientific or humane course of action, so we voiced our concern. The keepers said, at that age, the orangutan was all muscle and it would barely feel it. He likened it to hitting one of us with a rolled-up newspaper.

We asked how the orangutan would react. We were worried it might become aggressive and attack Pema, who was looking understandably anxious. The keepers gave a shrug and said they weren't sure, but it would probably be okay. Not the most reassuring of answers. However, we had to assume they knew what they were doing and besides; we were out of options.

Two of the keepers picked up a large tree branch between them and approached Pema, telling him to stand very still. They spoke sternly to the orangutan in Malaysian and gave it a whack across the back with the branch. It immediately let go of Pema's neck, scrambled out of his t-shirt, jumped to the ground and took off up a tree, annoyed but unharmed. It might not have been the most elegant solution, but it was certainly effective.

The relief amongst the group was palpable. We thanked the keepers and set off once more for the main road.

It had been a day none of us would ever forget. Certainly not Pema. His t-shirt was stretched and ruined, he developed a nasty rash on his chest and for the rest of the trip he was known simply as 'Monkey Boy'.

CHAPTER FIFTEEN

FIVE GO MAD IN BORNEO

Sarawak and Sabah 1999. Okay, I'll admit it. Some of this chapter comes from a magazine article I had published about the trip (the one that reappeared in the dentist's office). Not that this will matter, as very few people read the original piece.

To recap. Pema, Struan, Nguyen, Seth and I have been in Borneo for several very eventful days. So far, the trip has had its ups and downs. We've had an incredible encounter with an orangutan but have also made the recent, devastating discovery that Seth has lost his whistle.

Despite this bombshell, we ratcheted our journey up a notch and travel away from the main tourist areas into the remote jungle. After a day's travel, we arrived in Kapit, a small town halfway up the mighty (but extremely muddy) Rejang River in central Sarawak.

Upon arrival, we began searching for a guide to take us into the wilderness. It turns out we didn't have to look far as the manager of our hotel also ran tours. How's that for convenient? His name was Joshua, and he was a young Iban tribesman, albeit a very westernised one. He had a good knowledge of the area we wanted to visit, seemed like a nice guy, was very passionate about the jungle and was recommended by a hotel visitor (whom I suspect was his mother), so we hired him.

The next day, preparations began for our journey and we were shown an extremely well-thumbed map of central Borneo. He pointed to a disturbingly small area of Sarawak close to the Kalimantan border (not far from the fighting) and explained that this was the only area left in central Borneo which hadn't been logged. He told us stories of crystal-clear waters full of fish and virgin rainforests alive with life. Then he told us the price.

After some hard bargaining, we negotiated an acceptable cost and arranged to leave the next day for five days and four nights in the depths of the jungle.

The first leg of our journey was a three-hour trip on one of the high-powered boats that regularly travelled the waterways of Borneo. These strange craft looked exactly like an airplane fuselage with the wings cut off and a bloody great engine welded to the rear. They were fast, noisy, potentially lethal and extremely uncomfortable, especially if you were travelling 'roof class' as we were.

It was a blindingly hot, bone-shaking ride on the top of the boat, but at least we got a good look at our surroundings, unencumbered as we were by any sort of luxury seating that may have obscured our view.

The first thing we noticed was the devastating impact logging was having on the area. Huge, fully laden logging boats chugged up and down the river, and the forest wore long dirt scars where the trees had been ripped out.

In the river, massive tree stumps and rogue logs tumbled through the swirling currents. These half-submerged obstacles made river travel treacherous, and we were disturbed to see several sunken hulls of lost logging boats poking out of the river, pointing, bow first, at the sky like accusing fingers.

By travelling 'roof class' at least we would be able to abandon ship easily, although looking at the swollen, filthy water surging past the boat, that wasn't much comfort.

It turned out that 'roof class' was luxurious compared to our next mode of transport, the longboat. Longboats were extra-long canoes with outboard motors attached to the back. Josh had hired two of them for us. The first boat carried all our gear plus two of four non-English-speaking guides. The second contained the other two native boatmen, Josh and us. The guides seemed friendly enough, laughing heartily whenever we did something stupid, which was often.

The introductions over, such as they were, we set off upriver, spending the next four hours with our backs against planks of wood and our pampered western bottoms cushion-less against the boat's hard floor.

But we didn't dwell on our discomfort for long; there were too many other things to worry about. For instance, the log-filled river we were racing blindly along or the thirty-nine sets of rapids we had yet to traverse. Each set brought with it the possibility of, at best, a soaking, at worst capsizing, being sucked under the water and dashed against the rocks, then slipping into unconsciousness as our lungs slowly filled with muddy water.

We became used to the dangers of longboat travel. The low hum of the motor lulled us into a false sense of security, and the sheer depth and presence of the jungle stifled the will to talk. It was during one of these moments that Nguyen spotted three wild boars emerging from the jungle. Also seeing them, the tribesman driving the longboat swung toward the shore.

Suddenly, the guy at the front of the boat pulled an extremely basic, battered rifle from under his seat. In an instant, he flicked it up to his shoulder, took aim, and fired. The middle pig fell to the jungle floor. We were stunned. He had dropped a moving target from a rocking boat, at a distance of twenty metres, through trees, with an antique weapon that didn't have any sights.

There was much rejoicing as the pig's corpse was retrieved and thrown into the other boat (hot and bleeding on top of our packs). Josh gave us a grin and told us the pig would be our evening meal. He neglected to mention that it would also be breakfast, lunch and dinner for the next five days.

An hour later, we arrived at what was laughingly described as our camp. I've seen camps before and this wasn't one. This was a piece of tarpaulin thrown over a couple of tree branches with several logs of bamboo tied together to form an extremely uncomfortable platform. Another tarpaulin was laid over the bamboo to keep the insects out and that was it. I prayed the insect screen would work because, as Josh unloaded the boat, I noticed an extremely large, fuzzy spider that looked suspiciously like a tarantula crawling along the top of the tarpaulin.

I suffer from arachnophobia, and this did my nerves no good at all. Especially as the potentially deadly spider had disappeared. Probably the only things in camp more nervous than me at that moment were the two live chickens just unloaded from the supply boat. No one was offering them life insurance.

It was interesting observing the cooking of the wild boar; first, it was quartered, then the pieces were thrown into the fire to burn off all the hair. After that, it was skinned and gutted with most of the meat, cut into cubes, wrapped in foil, and placed on the embers for roasting. Next came the head, which was unceremoniously embedded on a stake and placed in the flames.

As I sat on a log wondering where the spider was, looking into the smoking eyes of the pig's disembodied head, trying to converse with Iban tribesmen who didn't speak English as they cleaned their parangs (large, very sharp machete-like knives), I wondered about the wisdom of our jungle excursion.

Looking at the other four in our group as they ate a hearty meal of burned pork cubes and rice, followed by pig intestine stew and roasted pig heart, I could see they were thinking the same thing. This feeling intensified when our guides returned from an early evening hunting trip with a frog. It was a very big frog, and we were told it would make good eating. Then, just to remind us how far from civilisation we were, the tribesmen grabbed the live frog and snapped its hind legs so it couldn't hop away.

Apparently, they are tastier when cooked fresh. After that, they said goodnight (I think, but it could have been anything) and promptly went to sleep. Sadly, this was not an option for the rest of us, unaccustomed as we were to sleeping on small logs.

I stayed awake most of the night thinking how easy it would be for our guides to slit our throats and bury us in the jungle. A creature, which I believe to have come from the Jurassic period, crashed about in the jungle next to my head at 2 am, which didn't help my insomnia. Finally, the morning dawned and Joshua brought us all a cup of tea. As this wasn't the behaviour of a murdering psychopath, I relaxed and we chatted amicably over a breakfast of frog on toast.

When we'd finished eating, we packed up camp and jumped back into the longboats for another posterior-pounding six hours. It had rained overnight, so the river was up and possibly even more treacherous than the day before.

Five hours and hundreds of kilometres later, Josh told us we were finally in a part of Borneo that hadn't been logged. It was an eerie feeling. The surrounding rainforest was noticeably thicker and noisier and the tributaries running into the main river were cleaner, or at least a lighter shade of brown.

The overnight rain filled the rivers with runoff, meaning that the crystal-clear water we'd been promised would remain a myth. This didn't concern me as much as the lack of wildlife on display. We'd seen a few birds, including a rare hornbill and an eagle, but I had expected to see monkeys swinging through the trees and snakes sunbathing on the river banks.

Josh assured me we'd have a greater chance of sighting wildlife when we got to our new camp. This didn't turn out to be so; in fact, the only thing we discovered at our new campsite was that it was even less comfortable than the previous one. A feat I wouldn't have believed possible. This time, the tarpaulin went straight on the ground. No luxurious raised platform for us. We were in the real jungle now.

After a disappointing and unsuccessful scout around for monkeys, we took a dip in the river. Josh told us to stay close to the shore as the waters were extremely dangerous. Being cocky, over-confident Kiwis, we immediately dismissed his warnings and plunged in. Within seconds, I could see what he was talking about. The undertow was incredibly powerful, and it took a great deal of effort not to be pulled further out by the swirling current. While we were in the river, Josh watched us like a hawk, constantly warning us not to go any deeper.

Pema, being young and reckless, took Josh's warnings as a challenge and became determined to take on the river's main rapid before the day was out. Struan, being older, equally reckless and apparently very stupid, agreed to give it a go as well.

I thought this was a very bad idea and left them to it. Instead, I did something more sensible, like exploring the jungle, ill-equipped and by myself. I told Josh my plans, brushed aside his concerns and headed off. I had a parang (machete) I'd bought in Kapit and a length of rope. I was prepared for everything. Or so I thought. It took me twenty minutes to hack my way to the top of the first ridge. Within that time, I had been ripped to shreds by thorny plants, tripped over countless times by vines and had become completely disorientated. The jungle was unbelievably thick and the only paths on offer were the ones you made yourself.

As I sat puffing heavily at the top of the ridge, I caught sight of movement ahead of me. Flushed with excitement, I crept forward. It was a squirrel. Not the most exciting find I'll grant you, but it was wildlife, so I followed it. After about ten minutes of squirrel stalking, my energy levels flagged, and I realised I was lost. I could hear the river behind me and turned toward it, convinced it would lead me to our camp. Unfortunately, my path to the river was blocked by a very steep cliff, so I took the only option open to me, and fell down the cliff. Fortunately, several trees broke my fall, and I arrived at the bottom cut, exhausted and bruised, but otherwise unhurt. Panting, I saw I was still several metres above the river, but seeing the water below me gave me some measure of relief. My joy was short-lived as I realised I was at the meeting of two rivers and had no idea which one our camp lay on.

I was devastated. I knew I couldn't go on for much longer. I was breathing heavily, dripping with sweat, and had no water or food. There was no point staying where I was, so I hauled myself to my feet, climbed onto a dead tree that spanned the banks above the river and walked unsteadily along its trunk. On the other side, I began slashing my way through the undergrowth, spiking myself in the head with a thorn. By now, I was bleeding from various cuts and scratches and too tired to care.

I stumbled over a vine, fell down another small cliff, and landed by the river's edge. About two-hundred yards in front of me, I could make out Seth standing by our camp. I called for help and was soon able to flop gratefully into the longboat that had been sent to rescue me.

I arrived back at camp amazed to discover that my tussle with the jungle had been the least interesting thing to occur that afternoon. In my absence, Pema and Struan had ignored Josh's warnings and taken on the river. The river won. Pema, using all his strength, struck out of the rapid and make it to shore, jubilant but exhausted.

Struan was not so fortunate. He was dragged downstream and sucked into a large swirling hole.

Seth and Nguyen ran after him, watching helplessly as the river held him under. Anxious moments passed while Struan battled to the surface, finally doing so but using the last ounce of his strength. Hearing the commotion and guessing what had happened, Josh grabbed one of the other guides and ran for the longboat.

Struan was well and truly spent, but somehow held on to an overhead vine for a few vital seconds before being dragged away. This gave Josh time to reach him and pull him into the boat before the river sucked him down for the final time. Exhausted, shaken and contrite, Struan was returned to camp. To his credit, Josh didn't admonish us. It wasn't necessary; we were under no illusion of how foolishly we'd behaved.

To lighten the mood, Josh announced that Struan and I had earned Iban nicknames. I became known as 'The Great White Rhinoceros' due to my complete lack of stealth in the jungle and Struan was aptly christened 'The Drowning Man'.

As I lay under our tarpaulin roof that evening listening to fat drops of rain dripping from the trees and the irregular snores of my friends, I thought about our jungle experiences thus far. Our wildlife tally was poor. We'd seen a wild boar (which we shot and ate), a frog (which we ate), two chickens (which we were about to eat), a squirrel (which got away) and a few birds. Our transport was uncomfortable and our accommodation basic in the extreme. Struan had nearly died. I was exhausted and covered in cuts and bruises. Nguyen had discovered an irrational fear of leeches and Pema was homesick.

But despite all of this, I felt uplifted. I knew that no matter what the jungle threw at us from now on, we'd be able to handle it. Because even this short time in the jungle had changed us. We now had the wisdom gained from experience, strength from adversity, and unity forged by a common goal.

And most importantly, Seth had found his whistle.

CHAPTER SIXTEEN

BATTY

Sarawak Borneo 1999. We're deep in lost diary territory again, so the content is courtesy of many phone calls to Struan and Nguyen (expensive, as Nguyen is in the UK, but I'm happy to pay for it to bring you a good yarn) and photos. They really are as good as a thousand words.

On our way back to civilisation (in Borneo, that's a relative term), we stopped at an Iban Longhouse to drop off one of our guides. Whilst there, we were invited inside for a look around and a chat with the chief. This was a rare experience, as this longhouse was very traditional and had never been opened to tourists.

A longhouse is exactly what it sounds like, a longhouse. They were traditionally built off the ground on stilts and contained a long public area on one side and sectioned off private dwellings on the other, with everything under an extended roof. They can be quite large, with some over one thousand metres in length.

The one we visited had the dimensions of six to eight standard houses linked together. It was made primarily of wood, sat alongside the river, and had a docking area out the front for canoes. Dozens of families resided there and the living conditions were very basic.

There was an eclectic mix of clothing on display, with most of the guys either shirtless or in a mix of western clothing, while the women generally wore sarongs or similarly light garments.

We were greeted by the chief himself, who had to formally invite us inside. As we were vouched for by our guide, he decided we were okay and allowed us to enter. We were treated in a very friendly manner, which was lucky because we soon discovered that, until recently, they had been a headhunting tribe.

The Iban were renowned as fierce warriors and would collect their enemy's head as a trophy or as proof of a victory. The practice was curtailed when a ban was implemented by the British in the 1800s but was revived during the Japanese occupation of the region in World War Two. There was also evidence of headhunting during a failed occupation of Sarawak by Indonesia in the 1960s and rumours persisted of the practice occurring in tribal disputes between remote tribes. Which was a bit close for comfort.

Evidence of the tribe's success at headhunting was proudly on display within a large cane basket that hung from the roof in one of the communal areas. It was full of skulls. Actual human skulls. Now, I wasn't quite sure what the etiquette was when shown a container full of the decapitated heads of an enemy. Do you give the skulls a friendly pat? Complement the bone structure? Pick one up and fire it to a mate with a rugby pass? Who knows? We played it safe and didn't touch anything. There were quite a few really old, heavily tattooed men watching us, and I suspect they had a very particular set of skills.

To mark our visit, we were told they would hold a smoking ceremony. This information was translated by Joshua, our guide, and he said we were being afforded quite an honour. The ceremony started with everyone drinking glasses of Tuak, a traditional rice wine. We'd consumed Tuak before and it can have a hell of a kick. I'd fallen foul of it earlier in the trip and the results weren't pretty. The spirit was quite raw, and we all knocked it back, trying to keep the spluttering to a minimum.

The chief then lit a cigarette, had a few puffs and then inserted it between the grinning teeth of one of the skulls. This appeased the spirits of the dead, who were clearly no longer worried about the risks of having a ciggie. It was quite macabre seeing the smoke curl through the eye sockets of the skulls in the basket, knowing that these were the genuine heads of enemies taken by this tribe less than half a century ago.

We were going to try really hard not to piss them off.

Our visit was fascinating, and we were treated with kindness and generosity. Not once did they try to decapitate us, which I think is the sign of a good host.

The next guide to be dropped home was the oldest of the crew. He was the tribesman who had taken out the pig with a rifle that was nearly as ancient as he was. At a guess, I'd say he was in his seventies, but I'm not great at guessing ages, so let's leave ten years either way. His home was a rough shack on the river not far from Kapit, and when he arrived, a very attractive young woman rushed out to greet him. I said to Joshua that it was nice to see his daughter give him such a lovely welcome. Joshua laughed and said that it wasn't his daughter, it was his wife.

Well played, old fella, well played.

Once back in Kapit, we thanked Joshua for, well, literally keeping us alive, and paid the rest of our bill. He was grateful for the money but also pretty relieved to see the back of us. He certainly earned his fee.

With our lust for the jungle well sated we decided our next destination would be Niah National parks where we could visit the world-famous Niah limestone caves, a geological and archaeological wonder. To be honest, we weren't that interested in the cave's historical significance; what we really wanted to see were the bats and the swiftlets.

We had heard that the caves were home to hundreds of thousands of bats and a similarly huge population of swiftlets. In the evenings, the bats would fly out into the jungle at the same time as the birds returned to their nests. When this happened, the sky would be blacked out by the swirling clouds of winged creatures, intermingling as they passed each other. Who wouldn't want to see that?

The caves were also known for the daring feats of the native tribesmen who collected the nests of the swiftlets from high in the roof of the caves. The nests, when dried, were extremely valuable as they formed the basis of the Chinese delicacy known as bird's nest soup. This centuries-old dish is one of the world's most expensive foods, as it's rumoured to have incredible health benefits, including improved respiratory health, increased libido and general longevity.

In my limited experience, I've found that anything that becomes an expensive delicacy usually tastes like crap. Raw oysters; yuck. Crayfish; overrated. Caviar; salty rubbish. Truffle; tastes like dirt. Foie Gras; not as good as a pie.

So, while we were keen to watch the nests being collected, a sample wasn't on the menu.

There was a campground in the national park, and that was to be our accommodation for the night. On the bus ride to Niah, we had a team catch up and assessed everything that had happened so far. Nicknames were confirmed and a new saying was invented called 'Waiting for Seth'. This came about because of the interminably long time it took him to do his hair. His dark locks cascaded down the middle of his back nearly to his waist and he wore it tied back in either a loose ponytail, or pulled up into a bun. No matter which style he chose, it was never a quick process, especially if washing was involved.

A typical exchange would be.

"Where's Seth?"

"He's doing his hair."

"Well, there's an hour gone."

A pack of cards would then be produced, and we'd settle in to wait for a freshly groomed Seth to appear. It didn't annoy us too much as it was all part of his Zen coolness, that and saying things like "I'd rather light a candle than curse your darkness". None of us knew what the hell he was talking about half the time.

Nguyen had a different issue. He talked. A lot. About anything and everything. Fortunately, he was also extremely funny, so he got away with it. While discussing all of this, we decided that, while we had travelled well together thus far, there were things about all of us which annoyed the others (unsurprisingly). I'm not sure who came up with it, Nguyen I think, but a decision was made to call out these traits and encourage/force each member of our group to address them for twenty-four hours—Team Improvement Day was born.

I was the first to be discussed. Apparently, I tended to moan when things got tough. This was a harsh call. I was quite a bit older than the others and while Pema could break out a somersault with no ill effects, my back, neck and shoulders often hurt just from carrying my pack. Still, I didn't argue when told I wasn't allowed to complain for the next day.

Nguyen had one of the hardest tasks, as he wasn't allowed to talk at all for twenty-four hours. Pema was a bit of a loner, so he was put in charge of group activities and had to take part in everything we did. Seth had the easiest assignment, as all he had to do was stop smoking. Struan was trickier. Most of the guys didn't know him very well, and he had been on his best behaviour, or maybe he was just nicer than the rest of us. No, it couldn't be that. Anyway, the only thing we could come up with was that he was grumpy when he had a hangover. It was decided he'd have to drink to excess that night and then be pleasant the following day. Pretty unfair, but Team Improvement Day was about tormenting our mates rather than looking for any meaningful personality advancement.

More on this to come, but first—to the bat cave (I've always wanted to say that).

The trek to the caves was quite difficult. It was over three kilometres in length and we had to follow a narrow, winding raised wooden walkway that twisted through dense jungle. The drop off to the jungle floor was quite steep in places and when you looked over the edge, you wondered what the hell was down there.

Borneo has one of the highest diversity of snakes in the world, with over one-hundred-and-sixty species, so there was almost bound to be some slithering around below us. Add to that nasty creepy crawlies and, of course leeches, and none of us were keen to leave the walkway.

A quick word on leeches. During our jungle trek, every single one of us ended up with at least one leech on our bodies. Often, we'd strip down for a swim in the river and there would be half a dozen on our legs and back. They certainly look disgusting, especially when swollen up with blood, but they don't actually hurt. We had been told you could burn them off and while that worked; it was pretty unpleasant.

Most of the time, we just let them feed until they were full, and they fell off by themselves. They do release an anticoagulant when they attach so you bleed a lot from a bite, but we had a good first-aid kit and were able to clean and seal the wounds pretty easily. The thing that horrified me the most about leeches was watching them climb up the side of our shelters at night so they could drop on you in your sleep. To stop this, our guides left burning logs in front of the entrance to our bivouacs and along the sides. The fire kept them away. There's a handy tip for the next time you find yourself camping next to a leech-infested swamp.

The caves were huge and worth the walk. The entrance to the main cave is over sixty metres high and over two-hundred-and-fifty metres wide. Stalactites and jungle creepers hang from the roof and the cave entrance is considered to be one of the most spectacular in the world. Inside, the cavern is even bigger and the thing that strikes you most are the precariously positioned bamboo poles and ladders that stretch to the cave roof—almost five stories high in some places. These are the scaffolding collectors used to get to the swiftlet nests.

I don't care how expensive or prized the nests are. There's no way in hell I'd be risking life and limb shimmying up a thin pole and balancing at the top while trying to scrape some scraggly nest off the wall. Every year, several gatherers are killed or seriously injured trying to collect the nests. There's got to be an easier way to earn a living.

We really hadn't done our homework before going to the caves because we didn't see any nest gatherers in action, completely missed the cave paintings that were in a nearby cave, and had no idea of the archaeological excavations happening near the entrance. Not that we cared, as the caves themselves were well cool, and judging by the amount of guano that splattered the boardwalk, there were bats aplenty. We could make out some high on the cave roof and excitedly positioned ourselves at the cave entrance waiting for the much-anticipated bat/swiftlet changeover at sundown.

On a scale of one to ten, with ten being 'holy crap, that was the most amazing thing I've ever seen', I'd say the bat/swiftlet changeover was a three. And by that, I mean there were only three bats and swiftlets in the sky. Okay, I'm being a bit harsh. A stream of bats did fly out of the cave entrance in a rush of wings, screeching and pooh, but there weren't many of them and there was a complete lack of swiftlets returning. All in all, it was a bit rubbish.

Maybe we just got the wrong night. Perhaps the swiftlets had gone to a movie, who knows, but as the sun dipped below the horizon and the sky darkened, Struan and Nguyen decided they'd had enough and headed back to camp. Seth, Pema and I stayed a bit longer, convinced that the main spectacle was yet to occur.

I believe that's called 'Eternal Optimism'.

It didn't get any better. A few stragglers pottered back and forth, but the expected maelstrom of winged creatures didn't happen. We finally left the caves about three-quarters of an hour after Struan and Nguyen. By then it was pitch black. There was no lighting on the path and we couldn't see anything at all. Seth, Pema and I only had one torch between us, so we had to proceed quite carefully, staying close together on the narrow walkway.

The jungle can be terrifying at night. It's incredibly noisy and the sounds are eerie and foreign. Something was making a noise like a high-pitched chainsaw and there were booming sounds and freakish cries that would come out of nowhere, distant one minute, then disturbingly close the next. Inevitably, some huge beast would be crashing around in the undergrowth but you couldn't see what it was, which makes it one hundred times worse. Suffice to say, we were very careful to stay safely on the walkway.

Struan and Nguyen weren't so lucky.

None of us had realised they didn't have a torch. Night falls fast in the jungle and about fifteen minutes into their trek back to camp they found themselves completely in the dark. At one point Struan fell off the walkway into the jungle and had to scramble quickly back up, frightened he'd fallen into a pit of vipers, which was eminently possible. He and Nguyen only made progress by using the flash of a camera to briefly illuminate the path before stumbling on, half-blinded and half-blind.

We found them both huddled together on the edge of the

walkway about a kilometre from camp. They were incredibly pleased to see us, as the experience had been extremely distressing. We all got it. The night walk had been scary enough for us and we could see.

Once we were safely back in camp, team improvement day began. Struan was plied with large quantities of low-grade liquor and quickly went through all the stages of drunkenness: "This is fun", "I love you guys", "Where's my shoe", "I'll fight the lot of you", "I'm going to sleep".

The next day he woke bleary-eyed and unwell, but to his credit approached the following twelve hours with forced cheerfulness, as per the rules. I also didn't complain, even when the boys gleefully announced we were going to play touch rugby in forty-degree heat.

This was organised by Pema, who was our tour leader for the day. Seth joined in, smoke-free, and Nguyen said nothing. The game nearly ended me, but I smiled, even when informed that everyone had agreed to play on for an extra half hour. Bastards. The only thing that kept me going was I knew Struan was suffering as much as me.

As the day wore on, Struan's hangover improved, Pema joined us in a raft of activities he'd organised. Seth chewed gum, while I was jovial and Nguyen remained silent, which was killing him. To add to Nguyen's suffering, we would torment him by saying blatantly incorrect things about subjects he was passionate about—Jean-Luc Picard was the best captain of the Starship Enterprise, Nickelback was a great band and Ridley Scott is overrated as a director. Every time we did this, he'd frown and scribble on a notepad.

Come the end of the day, at the very second we agreed Team Improvement day was officially over, Nguyen unleashed a torrent of abuse, reading from his pad and correcting everything we'd said. He talked solidly for an hour. When he finally stopped, we all agreed that Team Improvement Day had been a resounding success, and we'd never get on each other's nerves again.

That lasted less than twenty-four hours.

CHAPTER SEVENTEEN

A DOG AND A SNAKE-BEATING STICK

Sabah Borneo 1999. This may all be a fever dream.

I'm a stubborn and foolish man. I think we can all agree on that. So, when Struan, Seth, Pema and Nguyen announced they were going to travel through Brunei to get to Sabah, I did something completely different.

Brunei held no real interest for me. I thought it would be too built up and modern for my tastes. I was in Borneo for an off-grid jungle and wildlife experience and assumed I'd find neither in Bandar Seri Begawan. Instead, I elected to fly from Miri in Sarawak to Kota Kinabalu in Sabah, agreeing to meet the others there four days later.

I had no intention of staying in the city and as soon as I arrived; I jumped on a boat to the Island of Gaya off the coast of Kota Kinabalu. This was a luxury break for me. I stayed in a lovely hotel by the beach and spent my days playing in the crystal-clear waters of the Tunku Abdul Rahman National Park.

The ocean was bursting with life, including colourful tropical fish—Nemo and his mates, way before the movie was even thought of. I have vivid memories of snorkelling in the warm water, marvelling at the sea life and having a very small fish swimming alongside me, mimicking every move I made. It stayed with me for hours.

Whilst things were idyllic, I had a hankering for adventure so resolved to head for one of the other islands. I'd heard there were some interesting jungle walks and beautiful beaches in Pulau Manukan, which were relatively remote back then. These days it has a resort on it and is much more tourist-orientated but twenty-odd years ago, it was a different story. I was told I'd need a guide to take me on the trek as it was through the comparatively untouched jungle. That sounded great to me, so I booked a boat for the following day.

When I arrived, I stepped onto a long wooden jetty and began looking for guides. The place was deserted.

Seriously, there was no one around.

There were a few wooden shacks in what could, at a stretch, be called a town, but that was virtually empty as well.

What the hell was going on? Had there been a Zombie Apocalypse, and I'd missed the memo?

Finally, I came across a very old man on the steps of his house. I believe he might have been whittling. I can't in all honesty swear to the whittling, as I may be remembering a scene from a movie, but I'm sticking to it.

I approached, hoping he spoke English. He did, in a broken, hand gestures kind of way. We managed a mangled kind of communication and I asked where I could find a guide to take me to the other side of the Island. He shook his head. In an astonishing feat of bad timing and misfortune, I'd arrived on the day when all the Island's guides were on the mainland attending a guiding course.

What are the odds of that? I mean, come on. If I wrote that in a movie, you'd be like, bullshit, it would never happen. But happen it did.

I told him I wanted to go to a remote beach on the other side of the Island. Could he perhaps take me? More head shaking. It was a solid hour and a half tramp through the jungle to get there and he said he was too old to make the journey. I was crushed. Seeing my disappointment, he held up his hand, indicating for me to wait where I was (like I had anywhere else to go).

He returned a few minutes later with a lean, medium-sized mongrel dog beside him. He also had a large, hardened stick in one hand and a bottle of water in the other. I knew what the water was for, but the other two items had me stumped. He told me that the dog would go with me through the jungle, to make sure I didn't get lost and the stick was for bashing snakes with.

Things had just got interesting.

I held my hand out to the dog, and it gave me a friendly lick. I've always got on well with dogs so I couldn't foresee a problem there (Haha). Snakes were another matter. He handed me the stick and gave me a brief lesson on correct snake management technique.

Whack it in the head.

Even I could remember that. He nodded vigorously, pointed to the track and shook my hand. I assumed he was wishing me luck but thinking back, maybe he was saying goodbye.

Anyway, off I set with my dog, my water and my snake-beating stick. Not a care in the world and ready for adventure.

That lasted until the top of the first hill. It was hot; the path was overgrown, and the jungle loomed oppressively on either side of me. Maybe I hadn't thought this through. I was alone. No one knew where I was. The island was empty of potential rescuers, and the rainforest was full of dangers. The dog had no such concerns. He bounded happily ahead, following the track and turning to make sure I was following. I'd be fine, right? The dog knew what he was doing, and I was armed with an appropriate snake protection device. Yeah, I was being paranoid. I carried on, following my faithful hound, reassured.

Half-an-hour later, the dog suddenly turned off the track and plunged into the depths of the jungle. What the hell? If I lost the dog, I'd be stuffed.

I heard barking coming from behind the trees and then the sound of something large thundering through the undergrowth. Whatever it was belted past me about ten metres to my right. All I could see were shaking bushes and a blur of grey. An instant later, the dog appeared with a very disappointed look on his face. His expression clearly said, 'I did my job. What the hell were you doing?'

The penny dropped. He was a hunting dog, and his job was to flush prey out of the jungle. I called him over, gave him a pat and a drink of water, explaining that I prefer my prey unflushed. He gave me a lick, indicating he'd forgiven me for my poor hunting skills and I thought we had come to an understanding. We hadn't.

The track wound through pristine rainforest, verdant with a multitude of shades of green, and the dog and I settled into a rhythm. He'd scoot ahead, tail wagging, scouting the way, and I'd follow, now more comfortable with the sounds and sights of the jungle. Exotic plants bloomed on either side of me (I'm not a botanist, so I can't tell you what they were) and the forest was alive with movement and sound.

After another hour, the jungle opened up to reveal a beautiful, deserted beach. Golden sands stretched for several kilometres in a crescent shape flanked by cliffs on one end and trees on the other. Crystal-clear water lapped the shore. There wasn't a soul in sight.

I had the beach to myself. Well, not quite.

We approached from above, on the side of a bluff. I wound down the trail and entered a small clearing close to the ocean with the jungle behind me and a drop-off in front which fell a metre or so directly into the water. I took off my tramping boots and lowered myself down the incline into the ocean. The water was cool and refreshing and I waded in up to my waist.

I looked around, wondering where the dog was.

He hadn't gone far.

I heard urgent barking from my rear and a major disturbance in the bush behind me. I turned in time to see a gigantic monitor lizard burst from the clearing and head straight for me. The thing was eight or nine feet long and moving quickly, in full panic mode, with the dog chasing it. I'd never seen a lizard this big before. It was like a mini dinosaur with a crocodilian head and long sharp claws.

Monitor lizards won't normally attack unless provoked, but this one is looking pretty bloody provoked! They are known to be dangerous, with a powerful, venomous bite and a strong tail whip. Travel warnings say not to chase or threaten them, obviously no-one told the dog because he was doing both. As the lizard bore down on me, I froze, rooted to the spot. My options for evasive action were limited as I was up to my waist in water so I couldn't get out of its way even if I wanted to, which I desperately did.

Three metres away.

Two.

The lizard was at the top of the drop-off and hadn't slowed, its clawed feet slashing down one after the other, long tail thrashing back and forth. Without pausing, it launched itself from the clifftop, hitting the water slightly to my left, so close that the impact rocked me and a sheet of water engulfed my chest and head. The lizard's tail brushed my leg as it rocketed past, swimming strongly towards deeper water.

The dog appeared at the top of the incline, looking incredibly pleased with itself but once again disappointed with me. I spluttered and checked that the lizard was still swimming away. It was. I dragged myself back up the cliff and flopped down on the grass. The dog wandered over, unsure what the fuss was about. I gave him a pat and waited for my heart rate to return to normal. I couldn't be mad at my four-legged mate. He was just doing what he was trained to do and, if I was looking for adventure, I'd certainly found it.

I monitored the lizard (see what I did there?) and saw it come ashore several hundred metres up the beach. It stayed on the sand, so I thought I'd wander up and have a look at it in a less stressful situation. I kept my distance, not wanting to hassle it or push my luck. As soon as the lizard saw me, it ran for the jungle, but I was able to view it more clearly. It really was an impressive creature. Its hide was speckled grey, black and white with dotted yellow stripes, a smaller version of the lethal Komodo dragon but big enough to do serious damage.

Once it had retreated, I looked at the impressions its claws and tail had made in the sand, taking some photos. There had been no time to get the camera out before that. Leaving the dog standing guard on the beach, I took a final swim before drying off and preparing for the trek back through the jungle. The dog had finally realised I was a useless hunter and trotted along happily beside me as we wound along the track.

We'd been walking for about twenty minutes when I caught sight of movement on my right. A thin, bright green snake slithered out from behind a tree.

Where the hell was my snake beating stick? It was in my hand. Right, I thought, you've trained for this. Hang on. No, I hadn't. All that had happened was an old guy gave me a stick.

It's not like I was a seasoned snake handler. I didn't know it at the time, but the snake was a Sabah pit viper, which is highly venomous. The dog had obviously figured it out because when I turned around; he was nowhere to be seen.

Bloody typical, the one time I needed him to sort out some wildlife he'd run away, which tells you a lot about what I was currently facing. So, now it was just me, the snake and the stick.

I must have been wielding it like a professional, because the snake had stopped moving and was watching me carefully. I think it was a juvenile because it wasn't very aggressive, which made me wonder where mum was. I gripped the stick a little tighter, getting ready to bash if required, and very, very cautiously stepped off the trail and moved around the snake, giving it a wide berth.

I returned to the track about ten metres further on and a little after that the dog re-joined me—man's best friend except where snakes are involved.

Fair enough. That's just smart.

We made it back to his owner's house with no further excitement. The old guy seemed pleasantly surprised to see me. I told him of my adventures and he laughed.

"Hunting dog," he said and patted the hound.

No kidding. Perhaps he might have mentioned that pre-trip. Still, I was very grateful, and it was a day I would certainly remember. I returned his snake-beating stick (unbloodied) and then headed down to the jetty to await pickup. My mate, the dog, accompanied me to the dock and sat with me while I waited for my water taxi. It was very sweet, and I felt we had forged a strong bond throughout the day.

More likely, he was making sure I left the island and was going back to tell the other dogs about his adventures with the most incompetent hunter in Borneo.

CHAPTER EIGHTEEN

SWIM STEVE, SWIM!

Sabah Borneo 1999. While writing this chapter in the absence of any sort of written evidence, I wondered just how accurate my memory was likely to be. This is what AI has to say.

Memory can be both accurate and inaccurate, and it's difficult to know how accurate a specific memory is. Memories can change over time, and they can be affected by emotions, other people, and our own expectations.

Factors that can affect memory accuracy

***•Time**: Memories can become less detailed over time.*

***•Retrieval**: Rehearsing a memory can make it more susceptible to change.*

***•Emotions**: Strong emotions can affect how we remember things.*

***•Expectations**: Our expectations can influence how we remember things.*

***•Context**: It's easier to remember things in a similar context to where you learned them.*

***•Suggestive procedures**: Suggestive questioning can implant false memories.*

So now you are absolutely none the wiser. Thanks, AI.

I met up with the rest of the crew in Kota Kinabalu, or KK as it's known locally, and regaled them with my island adventures. They reciprocated with stories of their trip to Brunei, having visited the incredible Jerudong theme park, which is the largest and most expensive in Asia. They said it was virtually deserted, free to locals and they had a great time on the rides.

We weren't going to be long in KK as we had the rest of Sabah to explore, but knew we'd be coming back. My impression was that it was a vibrant, exciting city, worthy of further exploration. This would have to wait, as we had more pressing issues.

We were off to see a floating city.

Okay, so, city is something of an over-statement. We had taken a boat trip to a Bajau fishing village called Kampung Penambawan on the Northern coast up from KK. The village was built on stilts over a river, had no power or running water and was part of a very poor community that was seldom visited, especially by western tourists. We weren't sure what to expect as the owners of the boat that took us there seemed bemused we'd want to visit.

I'm pleased we did as it was a unique experience and one that is no longer available as the village has been relocated to dry land as part of the Keluarga Malaysia Hardcore Poor Eradication Program. You've got to love any government initiative that has the word hardcore (unhyphenated) in its title, though I'm not so sure about eradicating the poor. That sounds a bit extreme. Hopefully, it's just a translation issue and not taken literally.

Anyhoo, back to the village. The settlement contained more than one-hundred simple houses built on stilt poles, perched over the river, and connected by extensive rough wooden boardwalks. The homes were made of palm thatch and didn't look that sturdy to me. It was a bustling community, and they were incredibly welcoming. Kids ran along the boardwalks to greet us and enthusiastic homeowners happily showed us their meagre properties. I had to be careful on the walkways as they weren't built to contain the weight or lack of grace of a six-foot clumsy westerner. I'd already fallen off a similar walkway into the river when visiting a longhouse earlier in the trip, much to everyone's amusement, and I didn't fancy repeating the experience.

It became clear that the villagers hadn't seen many westerners because the kids were fascinated by the hair on our bodies. Seth's flowing locks were a massive hit. I had several kids stroke the hairs on my arms and legs, laughing and pointing at their own smooth skin.

The stretch of water that supported the village was sheltered and calm. It was incredibly picturesque, as long as you didn't look too closely. All it took was a glance into the water between the houses for that idyllic impression to be destroyed. The river was full of household trash. We discovered similar pollution throughout our trip and it was sad to see such beautiful places blighted by litter. On one memorable ferry trip, we placed all of our rubbish into conveniently placed bins lined with plastic bags, like good tidy Kiwis. At the end of the journey, we watched in horror as one of the ferry staff collected the plastic bags, carefully tied them up and then biffed them in the river. Coming from a country that tries hard to protect its clean, green image, scenes like that are hard to take.

While all the living in the village was done over the water, the community did own one patch of land and had made the best possible use of it. They'd turned the roughly one-hundred by seventy-metre stretch of earth into a soccer pitch.

It was on.

Two teams were quickly assembled. The first consisted of five vastly overconfident Westerners and a few village ring-ins. The second, old men and kids, including one completely naked ten-year-old boy. This would be a cakewalk. We'd all played various forms of the beautiful game before and considered ourselves relatively adept. I elected to go into the goal, as I was the star keeper of my five aside evening team, plus it meant I wouldn't have to run around as much. Nguyen, Struan, Pema and Seth fancied themselves as centre forwards and strikers and, against an opposition of ancient old dudes and little kids, a scoring blitz was expected.

It happened, but it wasn't by us.

Straight after kick-off, the naked kid got the ball and immediately weaved through our entire team without anyone getting close to him. He slammed the ball past me into the goal without breaking a sweat. The rest of their team was equally good, including kids who looked no older than five and men, who I swear had been using walking frames before the game started. They must have been born with a ball at their feet because their skill levels were amazing.

It didn't help that the 'pitch' was hard-packed dirt, wildly uneven, unmarked and on a slope. They knew every inch of it and could avoid the potholes and loose rocks that formed part of the terrain. It was Brazil versus Norfolk Island, David versus Goliath, and we got well and truly spanked.

The naked ten-year-old scored more than our entire team and I've never been in a goal mouth that felt so huge. I don't think I saved a single shot. So much for star keeper. None of that really mattered, as the game was played with style and humour and was heaps of fun. They could see we were completely outclassed and applauded our feeble efforts as if we were premier league players.

To be fair, football in New Zealand has always been a poor cousin to rugby, and we grew up playing a different code. I say that for pride's sake. In reality, we simply got thrashed.

I'd like to say that the trip to the floating village gave us a greater understanding of the social inequalities faced by indigenous peoples as their way of life is eroded but it really didn't, we just had a great day out, gave the kids a few trinkets and readied ourselves for our next project—saving baby turtles.

You've probably seen nature documentaries where poor little baby turtles are hatched in the sand dunes, then have to run the gauntlet of swooping birds and carnivorous fish just to survive. Well, not on our watch. Team Borneo had taken a bus to Sandakan and then travel to the Turtle Islands to save as many of the little dudes as was humanly possible.

Not that we had any idea how to do it, or even if it was allowed.

There were three islands in the turtle island group, Pulau Selingan, Pulau Bakungan Kecil and Pulau Gulisan, but only one of them allowed tourists to visit—Selingan. There was limited accommodation on the island and, for once, we'd booked ahead (slightly) and got in. One of the reasons for staying overnight was to see the mother turtles come ashore and lay their eggs. There was also supposed to be great snorkelling around the islands, which appealed.

We had briefly considered going to one of the Islands off the southeast coast of Sabah instead. Many of the atolls were known as spectacular diving spots, but there had been warnings of pirate activity in the area and while we relished adventure, fighting armed brigands was a step too far.

It was an easy victory for the turtles.

The trip to Pulau Selingan took just over an hour and was fun. The weather was fine, and the sea was slight. As we cruised through the ocean, we passed Bagang, which are traditional fishing structures used to catch anchovy. The construction looked a bit like bamboo scaffolding attached to a floating house. The idea was to place a large fishing net on the bottom of the sea and then use light to attract fish. When enough congregated above the net, it was raised, catching everything within. We didn't actually see fishing occur, but the structures themselves were interesting.

Pulau Selingan is the second largest island in the group with an area of eight hectares and was the first turtle hatchery in Malaysia. It's a safe haven for both endangered green and hawksbill turtles and the chance of seeing a mother laying eggs was high as they come ashore almost every night. The island was exactly what you'd expect—a green triangle of jungle flanked by white sand and turquoise-coloured ocean. It was the sort of place you'd be overjoyed to be marooned upon—hopefully without any of that Lost rubbish going on or Tom Hanks popping up to play volleyball.

We settled into our accommodation, which was basic but clean and comfortable, especially when compared to some of the places we'd stayed recently. Everything felt five-star after our jungle camps.

It was late afternoon by the time we were settled and the turtles weren't due on the beach until after sunset. With several hours to kill, we went snorkelling.

When we arrived at the water, we were surprised to see an area roped off about two metres offshore where tourists were supposed to swim. The sea was calm, warm, shallow and completely unthreatening, yet several of the swimmers were decked out in inflatable survival equipment. As Kiwi boys who had grown up around the ocean, we were astounded.

I understand people who are not used to the sea being uncomfortable with it and you'd be crazy not to treat the ocean with respect, but these conditions were more benign than a tea party in an old folks' home.

We grabbed masks and snorkels from a table set up by the islanders and headed into the ocean outside the designated zone. There was a bit of arm waving and pointing, but once they saw how confident we were in the water, they relaxed and let us get on with it.

The snorkelling was amazing, and the visibility was excellent.

When we finally left the water, we chatted with some of the other tourists while waiting for the sun to go down. Numbers on the Island were limited to protect the turtles and Nguyen and I played a game to see if we could correctly identify the nationality of the other visitors. He pointed to a tall blonde lady and said I bet she's from Sweden and her name's probably Helga.

The woman saw us looking and came over to say hello. The first thing she said was: "My name is Helga and I'm from Sweden." I couldn't believe it. Nguyen tried to pretend he had supernatural tourist-identifying powers, but I wasn't buying it. He was as surprised as I was.

That evening, we were taken out to observe the turtles coming ashore to lay their eggs. A group of us crept around the beach, led by rangers armed with torches. We were told that all forms of light had to be extinguished when we came across the nesting females, which was fair enough. I don't imagine anyone would want to be hit with a spotlight when giving birth.

I've seen it up close, and it's not pretty. When my wife produced our first child, she was appalled when the nurses noticed I'd become quite pale and rushed over to see if I was okay. I believe her exact words were, "I'm the one pushing out a baby, not him!"

Harsh.

I manfully waved the nurse away (after accepting a glass of water and a chair) and said I'd probably be alright. That's just the kind of guy I am.

Back to the turtles.

They take between one to three hours to complete their nesting. This involves coming ashore, digging a nest with their flippers, laying and burying their eggs and then returning to the sea. Quite a palaver, especially when you consider that hawksbill turtles nest around four times per season at two-week intervals, laying between one-hundred-and-forty and two-hundred eggs per nest. Green turtles nest three to five times per season, laying an average of one-hundred-and-fifteen eggs in each nest.

My wife only did it twice. I'm not sure what she was complaining about.

Once the eggs are safely in the sand, they incubate for sixty days or more depending on the temperature of the beach, then it's a mad dash to the sea. Interestingly, the temperature of the nest determines the sex of the babies. Eggs that are buried in cooler spots produce males and nests in warmer spots, females.

There's probably an observation to be made there, but I'm not going anywhere near it.

Selingan is a conservation sanctuary, so once the adult turtles have returned to the sea, the eggs are dug up by the rangers and placed in controlled hatchery areas. The eggs are then marked with batch numbers so the hatching and release can be safely monitored.

I can't remember if it was green or hawksbill turtles we saw on the beach that evening but I recall being anxious that we didn't disturb the mums while they were laying, especially as we were stumbling around in the dark. I also recollect being impressed with the size and depth of the nests, which I was keen not to fall into (see stumbling around in the dark).

Despite the potential for injury, it was an incredible experience seeing the egg-laying process, but it was the release of the little guys I was really looking forward to. That was to come the following day, as we were told there was a batch due for release mid-morning.

We woke excited, ready to do our bit for conservation and absolutely determined all the turtles released while we were there would make it safely into the ocean and beyond. This was despite the fact that, in the wild, only one in a thousand baby turtles make it to adulthood. Statistics be damned. To prove I'd learnt something on the trip so far, I reimagined the infamous snake-beating stick from my previous adventures to become turtle predator beating sticks (not as catchy, I'll admit).

In other words, we armed ourselves with driftwood branches from the beach, ready to swat anything that came near our self-appointed charges. The rangers and the rest of the tourists regarded us with bemusement, but we remained dedicated to the cause. Nothing was said because I'm pretty sure no one could be bothered arguing with the crazy New Zealanders.

The time finally came for the release of the baby turtles and we cleared a path to the sea, forming a guard of honour stretching from the discharge point to the shoreline—a distance of about twenty metres. The moment arrived and about one-hundred freshly hatched turtles were released onto the sand and started flapping their way towards the ocean. It was ridiculously cute. The boys and I immediately snapped into high alert, scanning for frenzied attacks from all sides and above.

There was nothing about, not even a seagull.

I guess that's the point of having a sanctuary; you release them where they're perfectly safe.

Not deterred by the complete lack of predators, I picked what I considered to be the cutest and most vulnerable turtle, named him Steve (my favourite comedy name) and vowed to escort him to safety. This meant shepherding Steve to the water's edge, grabbing a mask and snorkel and following him as far as I could out to sea. I'm not sure if this was allowed, but the rangers seemed unconcerned, so I went ahead and did it, anyway.

I knew the turtles were usually safer in the ocean than on the land, and deep water was less dangerous than close to shore. With this in mind, Steve and I swam flat out toward the depths. He was a speedy little dude and with me by his side; he avoided the predatory fish that were cruising not far away (if only I'd thought to bring a fish-beating stick).

Once Steve was about five-hundred metres offshore, I knew it was time to let him go. It may be my imagination (and I'm pretty sure it was) but as I turned to leave, I swear he raised one of his tiny flippers in a salute.

Regardless of the odds, I'm sure Steve made it and it wouldn't surprise me if one day I'm involved in a shipwreck and a friendly sea turtle carries my unconscious body to safety on his shell.

Thanks in advance, Steve.

CHAPTER NINETEEN

BIG NOSES AND BAR FIGHTS

Sabah, 1999. This is the last chapter on Borneo. If anyone finds my diary, please burn it immediately. Under no circumstances should you attempt to correlate what it contains with these chapters. I'm listing this book under non-fiction and we don't want a kerfuffle.

The team split up again.

Struan and Pema wanted to climb Mount Kinabalu, the tallest mountain of Borneo at 4095 metres. It's the third highest island peak on Earth and can be climbed without mountaineering equipment, which was lucky because we didn't have any. The climb would take two days and involved spending one night in a hut on the mountain. It sounded like a lot of effort to me, so I proposed an alternative trip to a jungle camp I'd read about. Seth and Nguyen were keen to go to the camp, so we separated, agreeing to meet back in KK in three days.

The camp I'd heard about was called Uncle Tan's and it sold itself as a genuine wildlife experience located in the lower Kinabatangan valley. Genuine is one of the words that strikes fear into the seasoned traveller (which I wasn't at this stage). It either means a tourist trap which has been so over-visited that it ceased to be authentic years ago or a really, really basic, no-frills, edging on a crappy, possibly poorly run destination where you'll probably catch malaria or worse. Uncle Tan's fell into the second category.

I don't recall doing much research into the camp. Had I done so, I might have picked up the following red flags.

This is from Uncle Tan's biography on the company website, which, to be fair, probably wasn't in existence in 1999: '*... he left the company and set up his own bookshop. The venture failed* (RED FLAG). *Uncle Tan left for Sabah. Uncle Tan tried many things in Sabah. He was a noodle seller in a coffee shop, he ran a small restaurant. He tried his luck as a small weeding and felling contractor, opened a provisions shop, he reared chickens and pigs. He even gave English tuition and attempted to venture again in the book business. All of his early ventures in Sabah were short-lived as he tired of them* (FLAG).'

Uncle Tan is also described as 'legendary'. I'm not sure who gave him this moniker, though I suspect it was probably Uncle Tan or his mum.

Here are a few other gems from the website.

We do however wish to remind visitors that set in such a natural environment facilities are not of a FIVE STAR Resort & SPA and are in fact Spartan in nature (FLAG) *but we do our best under 'circumstances of wilderness',* (The apostrophes are theirs. FLAG) *to make your visit enjoyable and comfortable.*

And in bold

Staying at Uncle Tan's Wildlife Camp is a roughing out experience! (FLAG) *I also missed this gem. 'Often, it rains in a Rain Forest and a Wetland isn't exactly dry.'* And under the charming heading *PESTS IN YOUR HUT (FLAG) '... rats and squirrels will bite through your pack to get at the food. Rodents also love aspirin, paracetamol and toothpaste.'* Good to know the little furry guys are concerned about their dental hygiene. (FLAG).

And finally, my personal favourite. In caps this time. *DO NOT SWIM OR WASH IN THE RIVER! Big crocodiles have been spotted on River Safaris. Crocodiles have been seen taking wild pigs during River Safaris.* (FLAGGITY, FLAG, FLAG.)

All of this would have been good to know. But we didn't. The first clue that we weren't going to be staying in a five-star resort and spa came at the end of our journey up an extremely muddy river when we found the sign for UNCLE TAN'S WILDLIFE CAMP. It looked like it had been recently charged by a rhinoceros, run over by a 4X4, thrown in a swamp, attacked by monkeys and then nailed to a tree by a drunk person. Not exactly reassuring.

From there on, it was all downhill. The accommodation was run-down huts, and when I say run-down, I'm not kidding. They looked like they'd actually been run down. A tree had fallen on the one I was staying in and it had caved in the roof. This didn't improve the already questionable water-tightness of the structure and the mattress I was expected to sleep on was wet and lumpy. The main 'chill out' area at the front of the camp was an ugly, muddy, debris-strewn patch of bare ground. I was less than impressed.

In defence of Uncle Tan, the area seemed to contain way more wildlife than anywhere else we'd been. Monkeys could be seen swinging in the trees, wild pigs sauntered through the camp (probably trying to avoid the crocodiles) and my old friend the monitor lizard made an appearance. The hunting dog would have loved it!

I was less keen on some other camp inhabitants—spiders the size of my fist. I'm not sure what type of arachnid they were. I think it was the genus 'Bigscaryhairyfuckers' regardless. I avoided them like the plague.

The main reason we were there was to see the rare Proboscis Monkey entirely because of its glorious nose. I believe this particular monkey was created by the comedy gods. Very few other creations, aside from the naked mole rat, come close to the pure entertainment value of this big-honked bastard.

I mean, come on, it looks like it's wearing grey track pants, has a potbelly, squats like it's on the toilet all the time and has a large, bulbous, floppy penis-shaped nose.

You can't tell me someone isn't having a laugh.

We set off on our monkey safari at some ridiculous time in the morning. Context: for me, any time earlier than eight is ludicrous. We cruised up the river, which was still the colour of cream of mushroom soup, and quietly approached the spot where the proboscis monkeys were supposed to congregate. And there they were, just as amusingly ridiculous as I'd hoped. Their noses were indeed farcical, and they were by far the most ungainly simians I had ever seen.

I loved them immediately.

It was a great morning wildlife spotting and Uncle Tan's completely redeemed themselves. Wait, no they didn't. I was tired and irritable from attempting to sleep on a sodden, clumpy mattress, under a roof that threatened to collapse from the weight of the tree at any moment, potentially crushing me to death. There was bugger all to do and crappy conditions in which to do nothing.

Seth kept himself occupied by doing his hair and Nguyen suggested building a raft. Given the crocodile warning (which we still knew nothing about) this would probably have been a very, very, bad idea. I'd had enough. I packed up my toys and went home. In other words, I left the camp a day earlier than the other two, in a bad mood, despite the hilarious monkeys. I'm not great when I don't get enough sleep and probably behaved poorly, though nothing was ever said.

Well, not much anyway.

We all met up in Kota Kinabalu a few days later. I was well-rested and in a much-improved mood. Uncle Tan's didn't get any better, according to Nguyen and Seth, but Struan and Pema had excellent stories of their ascent of Mount Kinabalu. They said it was an arduous climb but worth it. Yeah, probably not for me. Even with the squalid conditions of Uncle Tan's, I stand by my phallic-nosed monkey decision.

On our first night together in the big city, we hit the town. The five of us ended up in a popular downtown bar. We were having a quiet drink and a few laughs when we noticed a commotion near the front of the establishment. We wandered over and immediately saw there was a fight brewing. Two groups of young Malaysian blokes were getting all het up over something and the bouncers shuffled them out of the bar into the street.

We followed, curious to see what would happen.

There was a lot of shouting and posturing, with some pushing and shoving thrown into the mix. If this had been a fight in New Zealand, there would have been a flurry of punches, someone would have gone down and that would have been it (hopefully). Here it was push, push, finger poke, abuse, then more pushing.

We stood back and looked on, but our western features stood out. We'd been noticed. None of us encouraged the fight. We were merely bystanders, watching and chatting amongst ourselves. By now, the two protagonists had really worked themselves up and the pushy, shovey, stuff increased in intensity. At this critical point, Nguyen said something funny. I can't even remember what; I don't think it even had anything to do with the fight, and I burst out laughing.

One of the guys involved in the altercation heard me and immediately took exception, assuming I was laughing at them (which I wasn't). He came steaming over and yelled something like, "Do you think this is funny?" I was about to assure him I didn't when he kicked me in the thigh.

Now, I'm not an aggressive person. I don't like violence and the only real confrontations I'd had were in the line of duty in the police. However, if someone boots me in the leg for no reason, I'm likely to react. I hit him with a short, sharp uppercut. It was an instinctive action, but I'm a big, strong guy and he was considerably smaller than me so he flew through the air, landed on the ground with a thud and then scurried under a car. I think he'd expected me to react with some shoving, so copping a punch in the jaw came as quite a surprise.

I immediately felt bad, so I moved towards him, intending to help him up. His friends thought I was going to hit him again, so his girlfriend began battering me with her handbag and another of his mates leapt on my back. Struan reacted quickly, like the good friend he is, and hauled the guy off me. Then the two of them began grappling on the ground.

I held up my hands to the girlfriend to show her I wasn't trying to hurt her boyfriend (bit late for that) and she ceased biffing me with her purse. The guy I'd hit was still taking cover under the car, so I turned back to see if Struan needed help. He and the man who had leapt on my back were still wrestling, so I grabbed the bloke and wrapped him in a bear hug, pinning his arms to his side. He pushed against me, but I was stronger, so I just held him there and told him to calm down. After a few unsuccessful attempts to break my hold, he finally did. Once I was sure he wasn't going to spark things up again, I let him go.

He stepped back and immediately screamed, "Don't you know who I am?"

Struan and I looked at each other and shook our heads. Struan replied, unconcerned. "No idea, mate." His answer deflated the guy, who backed away, muttering in Malaysian. No one had been hurt (much) but there was definitely some bruised pride, so we decided it would be better if we retreated to the bar. Fight over.

It was a shame we got caught up in the altercation because it wasn't indicative of the experiences we'd had in Borneo. Almost without exception, the people we'd met had greeted us with friendly smiles, curiosity, generosity and welcoming good humour. I can't compliment our guides and hosts enough. After all, one of them had literally saved Struan's life.

Our last few days in KK passed without further incident and we enjoyed the vibe of the city and ate some fantastic food. It had been an epic trip and overall, the team, who didn't really know each other well, had gelled into a tight unit. Nguyen had finally earned a nickname. After an evening at a nightclub where he lit up the dance floor, he became known as Dancing Homer, as his styles were reminiscent of Homer Simpson. Not really an accolade, but meant and accepted in good humour. Seth never received a nickname. He was way too cool for that.

But he still had his whistle.

I can't leave Borneo behind without one final story.

During our time in the jungle, I'd got into the habit of strapping my parang (a large machete about half a metre long) onto the outside of my thigh. It sat in a black scabbard; I was used to having it there. On the day we were due to leave, I was low on room in my pack, so I strapped the machete where it normally sat and forgot about it.

I got all the way to the boarding area before anyone noticed.

This was pre-9/11, so when it was finally spotted, the main concern was that it would be uncomfortable in the seat and I was advised to put it in my hand luggage. To me, that typified the relaxed attitude of the trip and those simpler times. Fricking great knife strapped to your leg on the plane? No worries, just make sure it doesn't get stuck in the armrest.

Goodbye Borneo. It was something.

As Struan said for a long time after his near drowning—'Glad to be here.'

CHAPTER TWENTY

A LAKE TOO FAR

Samoa 2000. I present to you a lost and found article. The magazine it was published in was in my office under several boxes of receipts that I really must throw out.

My best friend Quentin and I had come to Samoa on a surfing trip.

Okay, so we were on body boards, but that's still cool, right?

So far on the trip we'd foolishly leapt into surf that was too big for our abilities and nearly drowned. I suggested a day off. Quentin agreed and suggested lying around by the pool. This didn't sound very adventurous, so I suggested some sightseeing instead. I opened my Lonely Planet Guide and found an interesting-looking lake called Lanoto. That would be fun to visit.

The guide promised me an eerie, pea-green Crater Lake filled to the brim with wild goldfish, which had been released by German soldiers during the occupation of Samoa in 1919. How cool is that? The goldfishy lake, not the occupation. The guide continued by insisting that journeying to Lake Lanoto was an experience not to be missed.

Quentin's response was disappointing. He made it clear that he had every intention of proving the Lonely Planet wrong. Rather than hiking in 35 degree heat to the centre of the island, he chose instead to relax at the resort bar with a cold beer in his hand. Even my carefully thought out argument of 'What are ya?' failed to have any effect on his resolve.

Neither Quentin's steadfast refusal to accompany me, nor the mocking laughter of my fellow resort guests, shook my conviction and I set out to find a guide to lead me to this 'highly unusual and little-known spot'.

As luck would have it, the resort owner's wife knew of a French lady named Chantelle, who guided people around the island. Quicker than you could say, 'Picturesque expanse of water,' I picked up the phone and met my guide in Apia the following morning.

There were two ways to get to the lake. The first involved a two-hour, hard-out trek through the Samoan jungle and the second was a relatively easy forty-minute stroll along a clearly marked track. I plumped for the easy option, after all, I was on holiday. As I was relating my decision to Chantelle, the phone beeped like a reversing truck, then cut me off. I didn't worry about the disconnection, as I had been quite clear about my requirements.

Hadn't I? Yeah, of course I had.

I arrived in Apia early the next morning to pick up a few supplies for the walk. As an experienced traveller of tropical climates, I was well aware of the draining effects of the sun on the mind and body. Well-balanced and sustaining food and plenty of fluids would be essential for even the smallest outing. Bearing this in mind I entered a colourful supermarket and bought a packet of Kettle Fry Chips (Barbecue flavour), some Twisties (described by Wikipedia as a cheese curl corn-based snack food product, completely leaving out the words 'delicious and nutritious') and a small bottle of water. That'd see me through the day.

Believing I was well supplied for my scenic stroll, I met a fit-looking Samoan bloke who came up to me and asked if I was the man who wanted to go to Lake Lanoto. He introduced himself as Willy, Chantelle's assistant guide, and a native of the island.

This was my first surprise of the morning.

I had been labouring under the misapprehension that it would just be me and my exotic French guide Chantelle, going to the lake —she giggling shyly at my rugged New Zealand wit and charm, secretly appreciative of my manly good looks—me delighting her with tales of my single-handed conquest of the Borneo jungle, as I casually brought down a charging wild pig with a well-aimed Kettle Fry. That illusion shattered. I climbed into the back of the car and discovered surprise number two. A squat woman in safari shorts, jungle shirt and, I swear upon my life, a pith helmet, grinned at me from her side of the car.

She looked almost exactly like a female version of Lofty from the television program *It Ain't Half Hot Mum*. "Hi, I'm Marjorie," she informed me. "I'm a birdwatcher."

The sun glinted off a large single diamond that had been embedded in her front tooth.

I was unable to reply. Words failed me.

Chantelle filled the gap. She informed me that Marjorie would accompany us on our walk. I nodded dumbly and listened with a feeling of impending dread as 'The Margester' filled me in on the first fifty years of her life. Apparently, she had retired early and spent her time travelling the world, looking for rare birds.

Marjorie had spotted over 600 little feathery dudes in her travels thus far, and today she expected to find several Red Necked Thingies and, if we were really lucky, a Greater Spotted Warbling Whatsit. As a bird non-fancier, this excited me about as much as a tax audit.

'Still,' I thought. 'How bad could it be?'

In answer, Marjorie screamed, "Stop the car!"

From her tone, I assumed that the Fijian Coup had spread to Samoa, and we were about to be overrun by armed guerrillas. Chantelle slammed on the brakes and I dived bravely for cover behind Marjorie's pith helmet. She, however, had leapt from the still-moving car, binoculars and notepad in hand. Evidently 'The Margemeister' had sighted several Lesser Freckled Flying Critters in a nearby tree. Marjorie twittered with excitement and refused to get back into the car until we had all had a good look at them. It was going to be a long day.

After about an hour of trudging through the incredibly dense jungle, Chantelle announced she was a bit lost. Willy laughed. Obviously, I wasn't in on the joke because I was less than amused, especially as every ten paces we had to stop while the bird lady made strange strangled sounds in her throat. At first, I thought she was suffering from heat exhaustion or hopefully some sort of trip-ending breakdown, then she explained she was imitating the mating cry of the Larger Crested Tit. There was no answer to that, so I backed quietly away, careful not to make any sudden movements.

Where was I? Oh, that's right, lost.

Not that I could blame Chantelle. There was little evidence of a track anywhere.

No wonder the lake was 'little visited', I thought. It was bloody near impossible to find. Sensing my disquiet, Willy announced he was taking leadership of the tramp. He declared he would lead me to the lake and sent Chantelle and Marjorie off in the other direction. 'Fantastic,' I thought, progress at last.

An hour later, my legs gave out. When I could breathe again, I asked Willy where the hell the lake was. He cheerfully informed me we were over halfway there. It took a few minutes for my heat-addled brain to register this information.

"But it was only supposed to be a forty-minute walk." I gasped.

"Oh no," Announced Willy. "That's the way the ladies and babies go. We're going the man's way." His words, not mine, just to be clear.

"Well, strap me into a high chair and swaddle me in nappies." I wanted to cry. Instead, I gave a short ironic splutter and hauled myself to my feet.

Twenty minutes and three falls later, we came to a fork in the trail. "Don't go that way," said Willy, pointing to an overgrown ridge. "The last party that was searching for the lake went there. One guy died and the other three were found four days later on the other side of the island." He explained, the cheery smile never leaving his face. This wasn't so much the 'man's' way as the 'potentially lethal' way.

Suddenly I began missing the company of the bird lady, annoying as she had been. At least she wasn't trying to kill me.

I was completely exhausted. My lips were cracked, and I had no energy. Desperate for food, I hungrily ripped open my pack of Kettle Fries and bit into the first chip. The salt burned into the cracked skin of my lips, stealing the last remnants of moisture from my mouth.

I forced myself to eat about half the packet, helped by the occasional gulp of water from my rapidly dwindling supply. Willy waited patiently beside me, obviously wondering what kind of deranged idiot ate snack food in 35-degree heat.

After the rest, I felt marginally better and dragged myself to my feet. We plunged back into the foliage, and I stumbled along in Willy's wake. I no longer took any pleasure from being in the jungle. I just wanted to get to the lake, see the stupid goldfish and get back to the resort bar. The niggle of hunger in my inadequately fed gut soon became a gnaw, and I asked Willy if he had any food. He didn't, but told me there was a banana tree just around the next bend. He was right. It was full of small, green, unripe bananas.

Willy smiled. "They should be ready in a couple of weeks," he said, helpfully.

"That's fine," I replied as I sat down beside the tree. "I'll wait."

But my torture wouldn't end easily. Willy cajoled me back onto my feet by telling me that the lake was only a matter of minutes away. That news and the discovery of a leech making itself at home on my leg got me moving.

After just over three hours of hard tramping, we finally glimpsed water.

It was a wondrous sight. No, hang on, it bloody well wasn't. It was a murky crater lake surrounded by rotting vegetation. I'd seen much better bodies of water in New Zealand and I could drive to most of them.

Still, how about those hordes of wild German goldfish that I now expected to see leave the water and goose-step along the shoreline, giving me little Nazi salutes as they marched past (the sun was getting to me). I rushed to the lake's edge and gazed eagerly into the water. My reflection stared back. The lake was completely devoid of fish. Undeterred, I opened my last bag of Twisties and sat on a tree trunk overlooking the lake's edge.

I broke off a small piece of the cheese snack and crumbled it into the water, reasoning that if there were any fish in the vicinity, they would be unable to pass up this tasty snack. Five minutes later, a solitary small goldfish arrived, nibbled at the Twistie, spat it out, and disappeared back into the depths. No eerie feelings of awe, no hordes of fish, no goose-stepping, not even a small wave. That was it. My pilgrimage to Lake Lanoto had reached its exhausting and bitter anticlimax.

Willy joined me at the Lake and accepted a Twistie. I sighed and an unusual sound caught my ear. Unless I was mistaken, it was the mating cry of the Larger Crested Tit. I jumped to my feet in time to see Chantelle and Marjorie cresting the hill, the Bird Lady in full warble. They too had made it to the lake and just to rub salt into my many wounds, they weren't even puffing.

I stomped my foot like an angry two-year-old, threw away my copy of The Lonely Planet and told Willy I wanted to take the baby's way home.

CHAPTER TWENTY-ONE

ROSE PETALS AND ROAST DOG

Hong Kong and Vietnam 2007. Conveniently, the source material for the following is from another recently discovered journal. Judging by my notes, I was, once again, planning to write some travel articles about my trip, which I never got around to doing.

Hey, I'm super busy (this is a lie).

Eula and I celebrated our twentieth wedding anniversary by meeting in Hong Kong at the end of one of her work trips and then go to Vietnam for a few days. We'd spend four or five days together, celebrating in Hanoi. She'd return to New Zealand for work and I'd stay in Vietnam for a further six days of adventure travel.

Since her tragic death in August 2021, I've struggled to write about these kinds of trips. Looking at photographs of happy times with her is painful but also cathartic, as it reminds me of the amazing life we had together.

We had a great night in Hong Kong, exploring the town and finding a small Cuban eatery in the main restaurant area. We ate great food and drank mojitos, maybe a few too many, I couldn't possibly say. A perfect start to our anniversary.

Upon arrival in Vietnam, we got a taxi to our accommodation, the Sofitel Metropole in Hanoi, a beautiful five-star hotel. I'd informed the staff it was our anniversary and, because I'm a soppy romantic, had organised some special surprises for Eula. She received roses on arrival, and the bedroom was covered in rose petals. The bed also had a sprinkling of rose petals on it, all surrounding a heart-shaped box of chocolates. We were informed we could have our own personal butler if required. I had some great ideas about what we could make our personal butler do, but Eula shot them all down, saying there'd be a very good chance I'd be arrested under anti-slavery legislation. I called her a kill-joy, then had a small sulk.

To improve my mood, she took me to the hotel dining room and showed me the afternoon chocolate buffet, which included a fountain of liquid chocolate. That (and the accompanying sugar hit) cheered me up enormously. Plus, I had a brilliant personal butler/chocolate fountain idea. Eula immediately dismissed it as highly inappropriate and not physically possible. Still, I had chocolate, so didn't really care. My wife had learned years earlier that the way to my heart was via my incredibly sweet tooth.

We explored the rest of the hotel that afternoon, discovering a beautiful swimming pool, which, to be fair, wasn't exactly hidden, and were impressed to find huge bunches of beautiful flowers everywhere. The Metropole really was earning every one of those five stars.

We ate in the hotel that evening and, over pre-dinner drinks, found out another cool thing about the hotel. It had a bomb shelter built under the bar to provide shelter for guests during the Vietnam War, or the American War, as they call it in Asia. Both Joan Baez and Jane Fonda took refuge in it during air raids on the city. After the war, the bunker was closed and sealed until it was discovered again in 2011.

Dinner was excellent, which was no surprise. The place was all class. Eula was right at home. I was worried she'd move in permanently.

The following day was a Sunday, and the weather was fine. The hotel lay just across the road from Hoan Kiem Lake, a large fresh-water body of water that's a focal point for the city's public life. Its name means lake of the returned sword. Naturally, there's a legend attached, but it's so frigging confusing, I'm not even going to attempt to retell it. All you need to know is it involves an emperor, a magic sword, several battles, a Dragon King and, unexpectedly, a Golden Turtle God. Shit happened, people died, turtles were deified, swords were biffed into the water and someone built a very nice tower.

There you go. All caught up.

The biggest issue with the lake was you had to cross the road to get to it. In Vietnam, this is an extreme sport. There are no such things as pedestrian crossings or, if there are, everyone ignores them. The traffic is crazy. We saw whole families on a single motorcycle and others so loaded up with boxes it was a miracle they were upright. My favourite was a scooter with a box tied to the seat that towered over the driver, but that wasn't dangerous enough. Oh no, there was a passenger perched on top of the box. If you'd seen it in Cirque Du Soleil, you'd have applauded for ten minutes. Here, it was just another day on the roads.

Eula and I stood on the side of the road waiting for a break in the traffic. There wasn't one. A friendly local told us the idea was to step into the traffic and walk slowly but steadily across the road and the vehicles would go around you. This goes against everything most Westerners had been taught. To step into traffic was to die.

Still, when in Hanoi?

I told my lovely wife we'd have to do it if we wanted to see the lake. She freaked out and replied that she could see the lake perfectly well from where she was. I told her to shut her eyes and hold on to my arm and that's exactly what she did.

I stepped off the footpath into the seething throng of traffic. Taxis, buses, trucks, bikes, cyclos (a Vietnamese version of the rickshaw) and scooters hurtled towards us en-mass. It was a good thing Eula had her eyes closed because it looked like we were doomed, but then a miracle happened. The traffic manoeuvred around us. It was a bit like Moses parting the Red Sea. As long as you kept moving, in a slow, predictable manner, they avoided you.

However, if you hesitated, or God forbid, stopped, then you

were likely to be in the centre of a multi-vehicle pile-up. It was not a good system and certainly not advisable for any one of a nervous disposition.

Much to Eula's surprise, we made it to the lake unscathed. Only when she felt the footpath again did she open her eyes. It pulls at my heart that she had so much trust in me (especially given my history).

The walk around the lake was fascinating mainly because of the young boys and girls practicing breakdancing moves, including actual head-spinning and Ali G arm crossing. It was like being transported back to the seventies.

We saw the turtle tower, and it was very nice. I also spotted some turtles in the lake. One of them may have been a Golden God, but I couldn't swear to it. No Dragon Kings though.

We made it through a second road crossing and went back to the hotel for a stiff drink and a lie down.

The next day, we saw the city from the traffic's perspective and booked a cyclo ride.

The cyclo was invented in 1939 by a Frenchman, with the first one appearing in Cambodia. The idea migrated to Vietnam and increased in popularity with engines being fitted in the 1960s to make them easier to peddle—a bit like an early ebike. Cyclos have three rubber wheels similar to bicycle wheels, two at the front flanking a seat for the passenger and one at the back attached to a bike seat/pedal arrangement for the rider. A canvas roof covers the passenger seat in case of rain, sun, spit gobs from apartment dwellers and vindictive birds.

The advantage of riding in the front of the cyclo is you have an unobstructed view of everything around you. Life in the city is front and centre; the vibrant sights of new and old Hanoi, the madness of the traffic, a cacophony of sound, and the smells, spices and sewers, the good and the bad. Your senses are assaulted from the moment the peddling starts until you finally vacate the seat.

The disadvantage of riding in the front of a cyclo is virtually the same plus being in the death-seat if you hit anything or anything hits you, which in any Vietnamese city is a very real possibility.

Cyclos only seat one, so Eula had to put on her big-girl-pants and face it all without my arm to cling onto. In a photo from the trip, I can see her mid-traffic with a very thin smile painted on her face. This isn't necessarily a good gauge of her level of enjoyment, as Eula didn't photograph well. She was a beautiful woman, but froze in front of the lens. My daughter and I unkindly called it the photo grimace and teased her about it unmercifully.

The cyclo shots are definitely more grimace than smile, but once we were safely back at the hotel, she said the ride was equal measures exhilarating and terrifying. A perfect description.

We topped off the morning with some excellent beef pho at a street stall, then spent the afternoon fending off hawkers and their knock-off Rolexes.

Dinner was at a hidden gem of a restaurant called the Wild Lotus (now sadly closed). The ambience was incredible, with an indoor stream flowing through the dining room and ornate ancient art scattered through the space. The food matched the splendour of the décor and we had a lovely night.

The following day, we explored. When my wife was involved this, generally meant going shopping. Malls were her temples and retail her religion. She could have shopped for her country and often did. I, on the other hand, can only handle retail shopping for about seven minutes but would bite the bullet, do it, and only moan sporadically to keep my wife happy.

Fortunately (for me), the mall was a bit rubbish, so we wandered the streets to see what else we could find. To my delight, we came across an open air market. Looking at clothing may leave me cold, but give me exotic food stalls and I'll mooch around for hours.

It was fascinating. Tables were decked with an array of spices I could barely comprehend. The colours and smells were extraordinary, as were the fruit and veggie stalls. I recognised maybe twenty per cent of the produce. I was blown away by not only the variety of goods that were on display, but also the volume.

The French influence was present in the form of baskets of snails for sale—at least I assume they were eating snails, but maybe they were pet snails or racing snails. It was hard to tell.

I also saw a bowl filled with live, long, thin eels and benches overflowing with a huge assortment of freaky fish.

The food on display went from the brilliant to the bizarre—a dog made out of noodles, anyone? To the downright disturbing.

Sitting at a table in front of me were three roasted dogs. I couldn't believe what I was seeing, but there was no doubt some monster had cooked up a batch of canines. You could tell by the tails. I don't mind the occasional hot dog, but this was going too far.

As a dog-lover, I was horrified and revolted. Surely, this was illegal? I steered Eula away from the offending table and swallowed my pampered Western sensibilities, realising that I had to respect that other cultures have a different approach to life and food. That's part of the reason I travelled, to get a wider view of the world.

I wanted an authentic experience, away from the tourist trail, and here it was—poached puppies on a plate. I didn't have to like it, but I had to accept it.

Regardless, I gave my golden retriever a huge hug when I got home.

He was going to stay uncooked.

CHAPTER TWENTY-TWO

ALL ROADS LEAD TO THE CEMETERY

Vietnam 2007. While the diary makes up most of these chapters, I do make the effort to research and update many of the facts and figures contained within the book. Thanks internet. Please don't sue me.

Eula left on a Wednesday and I missed her immediately. We'd had a magic anniversary, including romantic walks, great food and quality time together. I'm grateful for that.

Still, I was far from finished with Vietnam and prepared to explore the country by myself. Well, that's not strictly true. I was staying with a good friend's brother and his family that night and then travelling with a local guide and driver for the rest of my stay.

My friend's sibling and his wife were gracious hosts. He was a wine importer and took me on a harrowing ride through the city on the back of his scooter to a very nice restaurant.

Much to my distress, we didn't wear helmets on the bike. In an attempt to curtail Vietnam's terrible road death rates, a law had been passed making helmet wearing compulsory. This came into effect in December. With my usual impeccable timing, I was there in September and no helmet was offered, so my melon remained unprotected.

We saw three crashes on the way to the restaurant. This was to become a theme throughout the rest of the trip.

Here are some edited snippets from Country Reports—a travel advisory service.

'Traffic in Vietnam is chaotic. Traffic accidents occur frequently. The most common victims are motorbike riders and pedestrians. At least 30 people die each day from transportation-related injuries and many more are injured, often with traumatic head injuries. Traffic accident injuries are the leading cause of death, severe injury, and emergency evacuation of foreigners. Traffic accidents are the single greatest health and safety risk you will face in Vietnam.'

Well, that's encouraging.

The article goes on to describe some of the horrors of driving, or simply being on the road in Vietnam. This includes: Vehicles travelling illegally against the flow of the traffic, poor road conditions, drivers using their horns for no apparent reason, livestock wandering into the road, sudden stops by motorcycles and bicycles, speed limits completely ignored, drivers ignoring traffic signals, an utter disregard for basic traffic principles and no adherence to traffic laws or enforcement by traffic police.

It also advises that you're not even safe as a pedestrian as vehicles routinely drive on the sidewalk.

Night driving offers a fresh level of hell. Roads are poorly lit. Busses and trucks travel at high speed with bright lights that they don't dim. Other vehicles don't have any lights at all. And, just to add that last little twist of the knife, vehicles of all types often stop in areas of the road that have no illumination. Of course they do.

But wait, there's more. Emergency roadside help is *theoretically* available nationwide, but the efficiency of these services is questionable and, best of all, trauma care is not widely available.

In other words, it's a complete shit show.

With this in mind, I was picked up by my guide and his driver at 6.30am the following morning. His name was Thang, which I thought was brilliant. This diminished slightly when he told me it was pronounced 'tongue'. Still excellent. I didn't record the driver's name in my notebook, so let's call him Roger because, why not?

We were headed to Cat Ba, which is a large island several hours east of Hanoi, on the coast. Yeah, I know I just said it was an island, so logically it would be on the coast, but it could have been an inland island. It wasn't, but it could have been. Let's not be pedantic.

Anyway, we drove directly into the tail of a typhoon. Yep. Off to the usual start.

The main roads, such as they were, had become rivers, literally. At one point, the water was so deep it was coming over the bonnet. Did the appalling conditions slow Roger down? No, they did not. Am I going to complain about this? No, I am not. Mainly because we made it to the city of Haiphong just in time to get the boat to Cat Ba, so no harm (except to some wash-drowned pedestrians), no foul.

The weather cleared up beautifully, and I had lunch at the delightfully named 'Dolphin Restaurant', which is still in business. According to my diary, I ate sautéed shrimp, pork and rice and it was 'pretty good'. I stand by that review.

After lunch, I hired a motorbike and ride it to Cat Ba National Park where I would go on a jungle tramp. I had promised Eula I would not hire a motorbike in Vietnam. This was a lie, but to make amends, I resolved to wear a helmet. The man at the motorcycle hire place said I didn't need a helmet. It was perfectly safe. He had a large scar on his head. I hired a helmet.

My motor-scooter was a Honda Beast. This made me happy. At least, it did until I just looked it up on the internet and discovered I was actually riding a Honda Beat.

My testosterone levels have immediately dropped.

It was a twenty-minute ride to the start of the jungle trail and I arrived completely crash-free. I dunno what all the fuss was about.

The tramp itself was amazing. The trails wound through the thick, lush jungle, but this would be more than just a walk through the trees. My destination was a NVA watch tower that was used by the Viet Cong during the war.

It took a couple of hours of trekking through some pretty

sketchy terrain to get there, including rock faces with ladders embedded in them.

The tower itself was 'tres impressionnant' (French influence in Nam getting to me). It loomed over 15 metres above the jungle and its condition was .... decaying. Basically, it was held together by forty years of rust.

I was amazed there were no 'Keep Off' signs or barriers anywhere. Health and Safety was completely absent. I guess they figured if you were stupid enough to try to climb it, then you'd be no loss when you inevitably fell off.

Excellent. I was exactly that amount of stupid.

About a third of the way up, I remembered I get vertigo on man-made structures. After another third and on a particularly rickety section, I became annoyed that no-one was around to read my T-shirt. It had been given to me by one of my more sarcastic mates and said, 'I DO ALL MY OWN STUNTS'. At that moment, it had never been more apt.

I didn't make it to the top of the tower—see 'vertigo' and 'rusty as fuck'—but the view I had from two-thirds the way up was spectacular. The jungle was laid out before me and I could see for kilometres. Those NVA dudes sure knew how to build a tower.

On the way back, I concentrated on wildlife spotting.

If you've read this far, you'll know that in any country I visit, I set myself the impossible task of viewing an animal in the wild, which I have virtually no chance of seeing. In Vietnam it was a tiger, which, had I seen one, would surely have eaten me.

At the end of the tramp my wildlife tally was as follows: One large spider (and I mean large, I have a photo of it and it was way bigger than my hand), two lizards, one crab (Why was it in the jungle? Had I discovered a new species? Crabbus Woodis), several frogs and a millipede.

I note no tigers were spotted.

Had I done any research at all, I would have realised that tigers hadn't been recorded in the wild in Vietnam since 1997 and were probably extinct. Still...

The guide told me once we were safely back at the scooter that he'd been very concerned about snakes coming out after the rain. I'm bloody pleased he kept that to himself.

The next day, we headed to Ha Long Bay. The name means 'descending dragon', so I added that to my wildlife spotting list. The bay features thousands of limestone karsts and monolithic islands in a multitude of shapes and sizes. Ha Long covers an area a little over fifteen-hundred kilometres squared and contains about two thousand islets.

It's all very Jurassic Park and pretty fricking impressive.

I was going to travel through the bay by boat (funnily enough) so we picked up two other Vietnamese guys. I assumed the boat captain and first mate. I'm up with all the nautical lingo.

The boat itself was pretty basic, and I'd be sleeping on the roof. I hoped to hell another cyclone wouldn't show up.

As we putted through this natural wonderland, I really felt the absence of my wife. I'd see something amazing then turn to share it with her and, well, it was just me. I can pinpoint this as the exact moment I discovered I wasn't good by myself and certainly didn't want to do much solo travelling.

The boat cruised along and I breathed in the beauty and serenity of the area. Just as I was feeling connected and at peace with the natural world...

FAWHOOOOM

A nearby fisherman had unleashed the equivalent of a small nuclear device on passing sea creatures.

I considered telling them that the practice of dynamite fishing had been banned by International Fishery Management Organisations, but decided against it, as they were clearly heavily armed.

We moved away from the blast zone, then tied up at a floating village where I hired a kayak. I paddled around hoping no bomb happy fishermen were lobbing grenades around and got back in time to have a feed of fresh fish cooked up on the boat. Yum.

In the afternoon, my guide took me to a cave he said wasn't normally visited by tourists. This was probably true as no-one tried to sell me T-shirts at the entrance. The only people there were me and Thang. I was pleased to have his company because we actually weren't alone in the caves. Hiding in the semi-light were by far the creepiest motherfracking spiders I have ever seen. These abominable arachnids had a relatively small, round body and stupidly long, spindly legs, but, here's the truly spooky part, their eyes glowed. It was bloody unnatural and just not right.

It was a super cool cave, but having seen the spiders, I was also happy to leave. Preferably without being possessed.

I spent that night on the roof of the boat, checking myself for spider bites and permanently on the lookout for descending dragons, tigers and dynamite. I didn't get much sleep.

We docked the following day in the early afternoon and faced a long drive to Coc Phoung National Park, about five hours southwest of our current location.

This gave me a chance to have a good chat with Thang. It was most illuminating. I noticed that neither he nor the driver were wearing their seat belts, despite him telling me that forty-six-thousand people a year die on the roads and many 'Look out for that truck!' moments.

I briefly considered joining that number shortly after when the driver put a Celine Dion CD on in the car. Hanson was next. Call me a musical snob if you must.

Gritting my teeth and ignoring the unacceptable audio, I asked Thang more questions. I wanted to know why the girls wore long gloves on their motorcycles. He said it was to protect their skin. Apparently, Vietnamese men look for three things in Vietnamese women.

1.A nice body.

2.White skin.

3.A pretty face,

"What about their personality?" I asked.

They laughed. Not important.

Righto.

On several occasions, both men asked if they could find a 'lady' for me. I replied I was all good for ladies, thanks. The one I had wouldn't be keen on me looking for any more. This was met with good natured pats on the back but also a small amount of annoyance, as I assume I was messing with a lucrative side hustle.

On that note, they took me to someone's brother-in-law's

restaurant for dinner. I didn't mind. It was incredibly authentic. It must have been because you don't often see the word 'disembowelled' on a menu targeting tourists.

I ordered the festival of goat and it certainly was a celebration of the hairy, horn adorned dudes. I had it three ways, raw (hmm), fried and roasted. Bloody delicious, it was too.

In fact, I'd go so far as to say—the kids were alright. Boom! Comedy Gold.

I'm going to end the chapter there because writing doesn't get any better than that.

CHAPTER TWENTY-THREE

THE MYSTERIOUS DUCK WHISPERER

Vietnam, 2007. Congratulations, you've hung in until the last chapter. There's a bit of a wrap up at the end, but aside from that, this is it, unless I have another spring clean.

Thang, Roger and I arrived at the accommodation in Coc Phaung at 9.45pm after some hair-raising night driving moments. I'm not sure why they have white lines in the middle of the road because no-one pays any attention to them.

My room was five-star luxury. If you take away three of the stars and remove the word 'luxury'. The air conditioning was a fan that could barely muster the energy to turn.

I was hot and dirty (a bit like the room) so I jumped into the shower. It had three settings, HOT, HOTTER and NO MORE CHEST HAIR. I stripped off, jumped in, soaped up and BANG, and everything went dead.

The power had gone off. No one bothered to tell me the electricity gets turned off at ten o'clock. Super.

I used cold water from the sink to rinse off the soap, then

discovered there's no towel. I used a pillow case and mentally subtracted another star from the already dismally low base.

I soon discovered the first of the wildlife in the park. Mosquitos, the size of zeppelins. There was a mosquito net in the room (half a star reinstated). It took me several attempts before I was successfully ensconced in it and safe from the dengue fever carrying bloodsuckers.

I slept surprisingly well.

The next morning, I put away a traditional Vietnamese breakfast of fried eggs and set off for a two-hour wildlife trek.

At the start of the trails, I encountered a slightly encouraging though totally confusing billboard. At the bottom, it showed two people putting rubbish in a bin. Good, so far. Above them, on the left, is a monkey in a tree that appears to be wearing pants. Ok, I can go with that. I don't mind if the wildlife is well-dressed. The rest of the poster is taken up by a guy on a seesaw firing a rifle at a tiger, who is also on the seesaw. A math equation sits above them.

It reads: 2 - 1 = 0.

Now, I'm no mathematical genius, but I'm pretty sure that's wrong.

The whole motif is puzzling. Why are they on a seesaw? Who is the guy with the gun? Why haven't the two non-littering people performed a citizen's arrest? If no one's sighted any tigers for ten years, why is there one on the poster? Is mathematics different in Vietnam?

I was befuddled.

I set off, hoping to see fashionably attired wildlife high. I also harboured a small hope of spotting a tiger. Even if one had been shot, there should still have been another lurking around somewhere.

Instead of wildlife, I found large groups of Vietnamese students. They seemed to have mistaken the nature trails for the halls of a university dorm and were in full party mode. They were making so much noise that any fauna within a ten K radius would need to be deaf, blind, and physically disabled to have stuck around.

At one point, I met a French guy coming the other way who

claimed to have seen a large black squirrel. I didn't believe him. You can't trust the French.

At the end of the trek, my wildlife tally was as follows: One tiger (on the poster), one butterfly, one rumour of a squirrel.

Hot, tired and disheartened, I went for a swim in the camp's river-fed swimming pool. It was pretty muddy, but I didn't really care. It was wet. That would do.

I was the only one using it and before long, a crowd of amused Vietnamese students gathered to watch me. As I was getting out, a harried receptionist rushed up to me and told me not to swim, as the water was too dirty. Where was she ten minutes ago? She pointed to fish swimming in the pool and reiterated her belated no-swimming advice.

The fish seemed happy enough, so I figured I'd be alright.

In a desperate attempt to see some wildlife, I visited the primate rescue centre. It was interesting if you like monkeys, which I do. I saw Langurs, which are some of the most endangered primates on earth. They were cute, with fuzzy beards and big bellies. The reason their guts are so big is that they are leaf-eating monkeys with multi-chambered stomachs so they can digest stodgy plant food. They have a high-fibre diet that's digested over a long period of time. Apparently, they burp a lot. I must have a multi-chambered stomach as well.

I also saw some long-tailed gibbons. The keeper told me many of the monkeys in their keeping had been found in food markets, rescued and sent to them.

Humans really do suck, but then they also run rehabilitation centres, so there's hope.

A little later I went back to my room and watched a channel called NOW which, entirely without irony, was playing the Phuket Triathlon from 1999.

My next stop was Kenh Ga floating village. It is a small fishing village surrounded by limestone mountains and a large, winding river. It's not on the main tourist route, so it was refreshingly uncrowded and friendly. I tootled around in boats for a while and was impressed by the relaxed atmosphere of the place. At one point, I saw a whole family cruising past and the woman in charge of the boat was rowing with her feet. I have enough trouble doing it with my hands. Impressive.

The name Kenh Ga is less romantic than its setting. It means Chicken Canal.

There are two possible origins for the name. The first is that the hot springs in the middle of the village are used for removing the feathers from chickens. I'm assuming the chickens are not in any state to complain about their feathers being removed, so not the best foundation story, especially from the chicken's perspective.

The second is that the top of the limestone mountain is shaped like a chicken. It didn't seem to resemble poultry to me, but maybe it looked different in ancient times. Still, as far as back-stories go, it's not exactly Descending Dragons or Golden Turtle Gods, is it?

However, it wasn't chickens that caught my attention in Kenh Ga; it was ducks. Or rather, the enigmatic figure accompanying the ducks. I spotted him standing alone on an island surrounded by the little quackers. Hundreds of them. He was a solitary figure, backlit by the sun, a wide-brimmed hat obscuring his face. At first, he stood still. The ducks waiting patiently at his feet, then he began walking slowly away and, incredibly, the ducks followed him, keeping pace no matter which way he turned. It was freaky. He seemed to have a real connection with the waterfowl. A true duck whisperer. Of course, he might have just had pockets filled with birdseed, but I prefer the mystic interpretation.

According to my diary, we stopped at a 'resort' where nothing happened. Apparently, the receptionist was very sweet and practiced her English on me. Dinner was a rip-off.

Moving on.

My final stop was the Tam Coc Caves, a flooded caves system and UNESCO World Heritage Site. The caves themselves were amazing, as were the temples and altars erected within them. They were also the most touristy experience I had in Vietnam. Thang told me that scams frequently occurred on the boats that took you through the caves.

He said a favourite ploy was for the boat drivers/rowers to plead to have a drink bought for them, claiming dehydration. The drink is then put beside them unopened and sold back to the person who sold it to you in the first place. The same can could be bought and sold multiple times. Genius.

I was also told to watch out for grannies. Yeah, you heard right.

These sweet oldsters would hop onto your boat and attempt to sell you handmade tablecloths and embroidered goods. True to form, this happened to me.

A saintly looking woman approached with an arm full of tat and a heart-wrenching story of starving children. She showed me a photo of said poverty-ravaged family. This might have worked had the kids not been thirty and quite tubby. When I politely declined, she turned from a kindly old lady to a hard-ass saleswoman. It was quite a thing to witness, but I held firm and left the tour free of embroidered-crap.

The Tam Coc Caves were the final stop of my solo tour. From there, all that was left was the drive back to Hanoi. Surely, nothing could go wrong.

And nothing did. The end.

Except....

Thang, Roger and I had one final meal left together—Lunch. I asked them to take me where they'd normally eat, not some touristy place, but an authentic local café. They looked hesitant, but I was insistent. I genuinely wanted to eat like a local, or so I thought.

They finally agreed, and we journeyed to a place far from the main road. Once we fought our way past a pack of rabid dogs, we made our way into the establishment. Within seconds of entering, I knew I'd made a terrible mistake.

The customers were seated around a large concrete table and a space was cleared for us by literally sweeping the previous diner's food scraps onto the floor, right where our feet went. Even before ordering, I knew I was going to get sick. Not because of the food quality, but the unsanitary conditions would be too much for my cosseted Western system. I wasn't just out of my comfort zone; I was in a completely new dimension. There would have been more germs on the door handle than I'd normally encounter in three months, especially as my wife was a clean freak and our home was always spotless.

I don't remember what I ate, but I vividly recall furry things rustling through the food scraps at our feet. I also recollect Thang telling me not to order beef pho in a street stall as, he reckoned, about fifty per cent of the meat would be from water buffalo. Given where we were currently dining and the unidentifiable meat on my plate, this statistic didn't seem particularly worrying. Water buffalo sounded like a step up.

When we got back to Hanoi, I gave Thang and Roger a healthy tip and checked into the Sheraton. Despite my protestations of eating like a local, the first thing I did was order a ludicrously overpriced ham and cheese toasted sandwich. My thinking was that it might neutralise the other germs I had just introduced to my body. It's reasoning like this that scuppered a potential career in nutritional science.

The sandwich was worth every penny and, for a few hours, I thought my plan might have worked. Then the vomiting began.

I only had one more day before my flight home. Fortunately, my stomach settled enough to make it to the Hanoi War Museum. I'd grown up with American movies and books relating to the Vietnam War and was interested to see how the other side saw it.

The museum was an eye-opener. You were left in absolutely no doubt as to whom the victors were. The North Vietnamese weaponry was displayed heroically in front of a monument constructed from US planes that had been shot down. The final display before leaving the museum was a large mural depicting the glorious NVA victory.

Interestingly, as I walked back to the hotel, I noticed American brand clothing everywhere. I remembered the breakdancing Eula, and I saw in the park and observed American films playing on the TV channels and movie theatres. Guns and Roses and many other American artists were on heavy rotation on the radio channels.

It occurred to me it might have taken forty years, but in some ways, America had finally conquered Vietnam.

I was going to finish there, but I've done two entire chapters on Vietnam and not once did I mention that the currency is the dong.

It's the only place you can say 'Is my dong large enough?' without being arrested.

Come on. That's more comedy gold.

FINAL NOTES

As you'd expect, I didn't finish travelling in 2007. There are many more stories to tell, but I'm adhering to that old show business adage—always leave them wanting more.

Of course, some readers will have had enough, others will consider it already too much but I'm not really talking to them. I'm talking to those who appreciate a good yarn and don't take travelling, or indeed life, too seriously.

For the most part, this book has been fun to write. It allowed me to revisit places I hadn't thought about for years and chuckle anew at my often naïve and foolhardy pursuits. None of which I'd change.

Writing about my wife has been challenging. Memories of her terminal illness are still very fresh and painful but writing her part in the story helps me remember that for the vast majority of her life she was vibrant, happy, funny, tolerant, patient, and for reasons I'll never fully understand, completely in love with me, as I was with her.

Returning to my early years of travel also allowed me to reconnect with a number of my travelling companions. This has been fun and reminded me why I wanted to travel with them in the first place. Even writing this makes me think I should have included a mad surf trip a friend and I did to Bali, plus there's always the tales of Eula and my adventures travelling around Europe in a battered VW van to be told. As I continue unpacking old boxes and catching up with friends from around the world, I wonder what other travel diaries might be uncovered.

Really, that's my way of setting up book number two if this sells well.

In the meantime, cheers and safe travels, wherever you may go.

Glenn

ACKNOWLEDGMENTS

This is my first indie-published book, so (appropriately) it's been quite a journey and a lot of people have helped me along the way. I'll mainly use first names here, as I'm an informal sort of guy.

First, there were my travel companions, most poignantly my late wife Eula plus Devon, my lovely daughter and great friends, Quentin, Snow, Simon, Boz, Struan, Nguyen, Seth and Pema (the Borneo crew). Shout out to Nige, who is always fun to bump into.

When it came to making the book, the following people have been invaluable. Jo, for her editorial support and insights, Struan, Simon and Snow, as readers and suppliers of lost diaries, and Justin for reading, editing, laughing in the right places and coming up with the amazing lost diaries concept.

Big thanks to Scott and Leonie from Visual Evolution Ltd for the incredible cover artwork, layout and design.

If you've got this far, thanks for being a reader. We authors love you and it's the reason we do all of this in the first place (and money, though there's generally not much of that).

Also, a hat tip to all the unknown and generally unacknowledged people who make travelling so much fun. The friendly locals, the hospitality workers, the tour guides, the travel agents, and general good buggers who inhabit this crazy, beautiful planet we call home.

Apologies to anyone I've missed out. It was someone else's fault.

ABOUT THE AUTHOR

Hi. I'm Glenn, a freelance writer with four traditionally published books to my credit. Two about my misadventures in the Police: The Laughing Policeman and Cop Out. And two children's books: The Brain Sucker and The Bully Chip, as well as a book for young adults —Deadhead.

The Lost Travel Diaries of the Laughing Policeman follows on from my best-selling policeman books and will be my first independently published book.

I have also written for television and had a movie made—The Catch—which no-one outside of New Zealand has seen. Myself and my daughter have also produced a podcast called War of the Words which was a lot of fun.

Now for a bit about me. I surf. I play Frisbee golf. I read. I play guitar (badly). I like dogs and cats. Hell, let's just include the whole animal kingdom and be done with it (except those monkeys with the red butts, they're just plain weird).

ALSO BY GLENN WOOD

The Laughing Policeman is the hilarious account of Glenn's adventures as a police cadet from the time he first thought of the idea as a naïve teenager who hoped the uniform might attract girls, to his first nervous and calamitous months on the beat.

A multitude of disasters accompany Glenn during his testing year at police training college. No-one is more surprised than he is to survive, relatively intact, the physical, intellectual and emotional challenges of such a rigorous course and to emerge as a highly-trained, competent police constable. Well, more or less...

This is a warm and funny book that was a best seller in New Zealand but will appeal to anyone who loves a laugh.

Following the success of The Laughing Policeman, Glenn Wood completes the story of his rather undistinguished career in the New Zealand Police with The Cop Out.

Constable Wood was a disaster waiting to happen. He was the sort of cop who was happier helping little old ladies across the street (even when they were quite content where they were) than pursuing the perpetrators of dreadful deeds.

But if he failed to strike fear into the hearts of the criminal underworld, his superiors had a real problem on their hands. Never before had they been forced to deal with such a well-meaning but accident-prone officer and they hoped, fervently, never to see his like again.

From his early encounters with a less-than-impressed public, through the terrifying days of the Springbok Tour riots, to the gradual realisation that perhaps he wasn't cut out for life on the beat, this is the hilarious story of a young cop who created a severe disturbance in the force.

FOR YOUNGER READERS

Evil genius Lester Smythe has a black heart.

He's invented a dangerous brain-sucking machine that removes the goodness from its victims.

Now he's using it to rid the world of all human kindness.

But Lester didn't count on Callum McCullock and his two best friends, engineering whiz-kid Sophie and Jinx Patterson, the world's unluckiest boy.

The trio vow to foil Lester's evil plan but can they stop him before things go from bad to disastrous?

"Utterly engaging, fast-paced and funny" Magpies Magazine.

"A fast moving thriller for 9-12 year olds. The final chapters are a glorious tumble of climactic events which bring the reader to a breathless conclusion." Catherine Mayo, author of Murder at Mykenai and The Bow.

Nominated for 2015 Sakura Medal in Japan.

A year after they defeated Lester Smythe - the evil mastermind featured in The Brain Sucker - Callum, Sophie and Jinx are having problems with the new kids at Thanxton High. The bullies seem to be targeting them. And the friends soon discover they are in the middle of a dangerous plot for revenge.

Who is behind it?

And what is the bully chip?

Printed in Dunstable, United Kingdom

68482453R00119